Breakup and Bounce Back

A Woman's Guide to Healing
Heartbreak, Cultivating Confidence,
and Rediscovering Love
Krista Cantell

Contents

Introduction

Not all storms come to disrupt your life, some are blessings...

Have you ever been through a breakup that felt like your world had crumbled to pieces? It's a pain that's tough to put into words, right? Where the pain is so intense that it is hard to describe or hold back tears just thinking about it. The kind of heartache that can make you feel like you're drowning in sorrow. Well, you're not alone.

We've all been there, including myself. I remember times of breakup grief where I was just curled into a ball, thinking to myself, why did I deserve this? I questioned myself: Am I destined to be alone? Constantly re-running the thoughts in my mind and asking myself, what went wrong? Getting stuck in this cycle that feels never-ending with lots of tears involved. But time heals all wounds. It's just a matter of how fast you can heal your heartbreak before moving on to a better, happier version of yourself.

I wrote this book because I wanted to offer you a roadmap, a guiding hand through the turbulent seas of heartbreak. I wanted to let you know that your heartbreak and your grief are normal and that you need your time and space to recover. You deserve to shed tears, pound your pillow, and release your emotions. I am not here to judge you for that, but I want to help you expedite your recovery process.

Whether your partner broke up with you or you broke up with your partner, the heartbreak can be equally challenging to process. Maybe your breakup was yesterday, last week, or even last month, but that pain still persists. Sometimes, it's not only the pain of having to lose a partner and feel lonely, but it can also uproot your entire life. I vividly remember a breakup from a long-term relationship where I had to move out to move on. It was not easy; it took time and was mentally and physically exhausting.

Navigating the pain of a breakup is one of the most profound emotional challenges we face. It often feels like the world has come to a standstill in these moments, leaving us stuck in our thoughts, fears, and tears. It's completely natural to feel this way, and I deeply understand the weight of this sorrow. Please remember, though, that every experience, no matter how painful, teaches us something valuable.

The universe may have a different plan for you, one that leads you to a love that truly resonates with your soul. It might be hard to see now, but you'll rediscover the vibrant spirit within you with time. And someday, when you least expect it, you might find yourself feeling that exhilarating joy and excitement once again as if you were experiencing the thrill of young love all over again. Remember, you deserve a love that celebrates every part of you.

Are you ready to begin your healing process?

So, here's the solution: You need to start by understanding yourself – your attachment style, unique breakup experience, and "breakup symptoms." And from that self-awareness, you can create your personalized roadmap to recovery and healing.

That's where this book comes in. It offers a transformative **"RECOVER"** framework tailor-made for you. With it, you will:

Reflect on the Pain

Now, let's take a look at the first step of the RECOVER framework. Understanding the emotional impact of heartbreak is like shining a light on the darkest corners of your heart. It's about more than just acknowledging the pain; it's about recognizing the deep emotional wounds, the scars, and the unique challenges your breakup has thrown your way. When you gain these insights, you're not just taking the first step towards healing – you're starting a profound transformation.

Emerging From the Heartbreak

The "Emerging From the Heartbreak" stage is a journey in itself. It's about navigating through the stormy post-breakup waters, addressing the challenges that may have caught you off guard, from handling the complexities of social media, where memories and emotions are intertwined, to coping with the profound loneliness that often follows a breakup. It's a journey of rebuilding connections – with friends, family, and, most importantly, with yourself.

Coping and Healing

As you move forward, you'll encounter immediate emotional distress. It's a turbulent sea that can sometimes feel overwhelming. Coping and healing involve more than just weathering the storm. It's about practicing mindfulness, being present at the moment, and setting boundaries that protect your heart. By doing so, you'll initiate the healing journey and start to regain control over your life.

Overcoming a Deeper Pain

This step, "Overcoming a Deeper Pain," is like a deep dive into your emotional well-being. It's about exploring strategies for long-term emotional healing. Therapy is a powerful tool that can help you process your emotions and develop coping strategies. Self-care becomes your companion as you prioritize your own well-being. You'll also focus on enhancing your emotional intelligence, which is crucial for building healthier relationships and lasting emotional resilience.

Venturing Into Self-Rediscovery

The journey of healing is also about rediscovering who you are. The "Venturing Into Self-Rediscovery" stage is where you reignite your passions, reconnect with forgotten dreams, and delve into personal growth. It's a profound exploration of your interests, talents, and the other things you may have put on hold. This stage involves uncovering a deeper sense of purpose and fulfillment in your life.

Empowering Self Belief

Your self-confidence might have taken a hit during your heartbreak. "Empowering Self Belief" is all about building it back up. Through exercises and challenges, you'll prepare for a more confident future. You'll rekindle the belief in yourself and your abilities, which is essential for stepping into new beginnings with grace and self-assuredness.

Reconnecting for New Beginnings

Lastly, "Reconnecting for New Beginnings" is about preparing yourself to re-enter the dating world. It's about more than just getting back out there; it's about doing so with a deep sense of self-awareness. You'll understand your attachment styles, recognize your readiness for new relationships, and engage in self-awareness exercises that empower you to form healthier and more meaningful connections in the future.

Each stage in the RECOVER framework is a building block for your transformation. They're your roadmap to healing, helping you overcome the pain of your past relationship and guiding you toward a brighter, happier future. The journey will take time, but as you progress through these stages, you'll find yourself in a much better place than you ever thought possible.

But what makes the RECOVER framework stand out? It's not a one-size-fits-all solution. Instead, it empowers you to reflect on your unique experience and "breakup symptoms" before crafting your unique recovery approach. This framework goes beyond clichéd and generic advice, offering interactive activities, practical solutions, and relatable stories to guide your healing journey.

The best part? It works. I've witnessed incredible transformations – women who've regained their confidence rebuilt their lives, and ventured into new, healthier relationships.

The benefits of this book are enormous.

- Gain clarity and understanding of your emotional turmoil, empowering you to take actionable steps toward healing and emotional well-being.

- Navigate post-breakup challenges confidently, building resilience during challenging times and preparing for future life transitions with greater ease.

- Manage immediate emotional distress more effectively, enhancing your overall quality of life and the ability to cope with adversity.

- Rebuild self-confidence and self-esteem, fueling your motivation for personal growth and happiness.

- Rediscover yourself and experience personal growth, igniting a deeper sense of purpose and fulfillment in life.

- Prepare for new relationships with self-awareness, equipping you to form healthier and more meaningful connections in the future.

- Enhance your emotional intelligence for lasting healing, fostering healthier relationships and ongoing emotional resilience.

- Develop a personalized roadmap to healing, ensuring active involvement in your healing journey for greater effectiveness and meaning.

- Reconnect with forgotten dreams and interests, infusing life with renewed purpose and satisfaction.

This book is not just a book; it's a promise of healing, renewal, and a brighter future. It's the guide you've been searching for – a shortcut to a better life filled with self-confidence, self-discovery, and the excitement of new beginnings.

1

Reflecting On The Pain

In the early days after a breakup, it often feels like the world has come crashing down around you. The person who once held a special place in your heart is suddenly gone, and you're left to grapple with a whirlwind of emotions. It's essential to understand that this is a natural part of the healing process and that you're not alone in your experience. This chapter dives deep into the emotional rollercoaster of heartbreak, helping you make sense of the whirlwind of feelings you're going through.

The Storm Within

Heartbreak is a storm within your heart and mind. It's a rollercoaster of emotions that can be difficult to navigate. In the initial stages, feeling overwhelmed, confused, and lost is common. Your feelings may swing from anger and sadness to nostalgia and even relief at times. This emotional turbulence can be intense, making you question your sanity and wonder if you'll ever regain your emotional footing.

The Anatomy of Heartbreak

Heartbreak isn't a single emotion; it's a complex mixture of feelings that manifest in various ways. Here's a closer look at the different emotions you may encounter:

Sadness: This is the most common emotion associated with a breakup. You mourn the loss of the relationship and the dreams you had for the future.

Anger: Feelings of frustration and resentment can surface. You might be angry at your ex-partner, yourself, or the situation.

Guilt: It's not uncommon to feel guilty for things that happened or didn't happen in the relationship. You might wonder if you could have done something differently.

Fear: The uncertainty of the future can be daunting. You may fear being alone, the unknown, or whether you'll ever find love again.

Nostalgia: You may find yourself reminiscing about the good times and idealizing your past relationship.

Relief: Paradoxically, you might also feel relief that the relationship has ended, especially if it was toxic or unsatisfying.

The Power of Acknowledgment

It's essential to acknowledge and embrace these emotions, no matter how uncomfortable they may be. Pretending they don't exist or suppressing them can only prolong the healing process. Instead, take the time to understand and accept what you're going through. Recognize that it's okay to feel these emotions and that they are a part of your journey toward healing. Once you start to accept your feelings, you will know that you are on the right path.

Finding Common Ground

What's comforting to know is that you're not alone in this journey. Heartbreak is a universal human experience. Everyone has felt the pangs of a shattered heart at some point in their lives. This shared experience is a reminder that you can and will overcome this pain. In the chapters to come, we'll explore the various stages of healing and the strategies that can help you rebuild your life after heartbreak.

This chapter is just the beginning of your journey. It's about understanding the emotional turbulence of heartbreak, acknowledging its presence, and finding solace in the fact that you are not alone. Remember, it's okay to feel lost and hurt right now. You're on a path of self-discovery and healing that, in time, will lead to a brighter future.

Insights into the Emotional Turmoil of Heartbreak

In the depths of heartbreak, the emotional turmoil can be overwhelming. It's as if you've been thrust into a storm of emotions with no clear path to navigate. This chapter delves deeper into the emotional rollercoaster of heartbreak, offering insights into the intense and often conflicting feelings that come with the territory.

The Raw Grief
Grief is at the heart of every breakup. The profound sorrow and sense of loss can make even the simplest tasks seem insurmountable. I can recall trying to go to work after a breakup but being unable to be productive because my mind was consumed with negative thoughts and sadness. During this time, it's important to remember that grief is not a linear process. It ebbs and flows like waves crashing on the shore. Some days, you might feel like you're starting to heal, only to be swept away by grief's powerful undertow the next. This is perfectly normal.

The Weight of Sadness
The sadness that accompanies a breakup can be soul-crushing. It's the tears you shed when you least expect them, the heaviness in your chest, and the emptiness you feel when you wake up. You

cannot merely wish this sadness away, but understanding that it's a natural response to loss can provide some comfort.

The Endless Questions

In the aftermath of a breakup, questions may plague your mind. "What went wrong?" "Could I have done something differently?" "Will I ever find love again?" These questions can be like a never-ending carousel, spinning through your thoughts day and night. It's important to realize that these questions are part of the process but don't necessarily need immediate answers.

The Unpredictable Anger

Anger is another emotion that often surfaces during heartbreak. It can be directed towards your ex-partner, yourself, or the universe for the unfairness of it all. It's essential to allow yourself to feel this anger but also to find healthy outlets for it, like journaling, talking with a friend, or seeking therapy.

The Guilt Trip

Guilt can be a heavy burden to bear after a breakup. You might replay past decisions and actions, wondering if you could have prevented the end of the relationship. Remember that relationships are a two-way street, and it's rarely the fault of just one person. It's important to forgive yourself for any mistakes and understand that growth comes from learning, not self-blame.

The Fear of the Unknown

The future can seem like a daunting and scary place after a breakup. The fear of being alone, the uncertainty of what lies ahead, and the apprehension about starting over can be paralyzing. However, it's crucial to remember that new beginnings are often born from endings, and the unknown can hold beautiful surprises.

The Longing for the Past

Nostalgia is a powerful emotion that can pull you back into memories of better times in the relationship. While it's expected that we cherish the good moments, it's essential to acknowledge that these moments were just one part of the overall picture. The relationship ended for a reason, and healing involves looking forward, not backward.

The Unexpected Relief
Strangely, you may also experience moments of relief after a breakup, especially if the relationship was unhealthy or unfulfilling. It's like a weight has been lifted, and you can breathe freely again. These moments of relief are an essential sign that you're on a path toward healing and rediscovery.

Understanding these emotional aspects of heartbreak is the first step towards managing and eventually overcoming them. In the chapters ahead, we'll explore strategies and insights to help you navigate this tumultuous journey and emerge stronger on the other side. Remember, healing from heartbreak is a process, and feeling all these emotions is okay. You're not alone, and there is hope for brighter days ahead.

Breakups Just Hit Different for Women

Breaking up is never easy, and the storm of emotions that follow affects both men and women. However, there are often distinct differences in how women process breakups. Let's take a closer look at some of those differences.

The Power of Connection
Women tend to place a significant emphasis on emotional connection in relationships. They often invest deeply in the emotional bonds they create with their partners. As a result, when a breakup occurs, the sense of loss can be particularly profound. It's not just the loss of the person but also the loss of a deep emotional connection that can take a significant toll.

The Need for Communication

Many women often feel a deep desire to discuss their feelings and experiences. Sharing their breakup journey with close friends and confidantes can be healing. This open and honest communication allows them to process their emotions and find support from their social circle. It's not necessarily about finding solutions; it's about seeking comfort in knowing that they are heard and understood.

Emotional Expressiveness

Women may be more emotionally expressive than men. This means they may readily show their feelings, such as crying, venting, or discussing their emotional state. This emotional release can be an essential part of the healing process, allowing women to release pent-up emotions and start the journey toward closure.

Seeking Closure

Women often seek closure more actively than men. They may want to have conversations with their ex-partners to better understand why the relationship ended. This quest for closure can help them understand the breakup and find a sense of resolution.

Self-Reflection and Growth

Women tend to engage in more self-reflection and introspection after a breakup. They often take the time to evaluate the relationship and consider how it has shaped them. This introspection can lead to personal growth and a deeper understanding of themselves and their desires in future relationships.

Emotional Resilience

Despite the emotional intensity of breakups, women often demonstrate remarkable resilience. They can bounce back, learn from their experiences, and become even stronger as a result. The ability to embrace vulnerability and use it as a stepping stone to personal growth is a unique characteristic of many women.

Support Systems

Women tend to rely on their support systems more readily than men. Friends, family, and therapists play a crucial role in helping women process their emotions and find solace during a breakup. This strong social network can be a powerful source of healing and strength.

Looking Ahead

One distinctive aspect of how women process breakups is their tendency to look to the future with optimism. Even amid heartbreak, many women begin to plan for what lies ahead. They focus on personal goals, self-care, and, often, new beginnings. Remember, you may not be a superwoman, but you are a superwoman who has the skills to bounce back and find a better version of yourself.

It's important to remember that these differences are not universal. People, regardless of gender, have unique ways of coping with breakups. The key is to honor and understand your individual process and embrace the best strategies for you.

In the chapters ahead, we will explore various coping strategies to help women navigate the turbulent waters of heartbreak and emerge stronger, wiser, and ready to embrace a new chapter in life. Remember, healing is a personal journey; there is no one-size-fits-all approach. You are strong, resilient, and capable of moving forward, regardless of your unique path.

Understanding the Physical Toll of Heartbreak

The pain of heartbreak isn't just emotional; it can also take a significant physical toll on your body. The mind-body connection is powerful, and when you're going through heartbreak, your body can experience a range of physical symptoms. Let's go ahead and break some of them down into more detail.

Stress on the Body

When you go through a breakup, your body goes into a state of stress. The emotional turmoil triggers the release of stress hormones like cortisol, which can have various physical effects. This heightened stress response can lead to increased heart rate, elevated blood pressure, and even muscle tension. The more significant problem is that this stress, if left unmanaged, can trigger unhealthy coping mechanisms like overeating or neglecting self-care, leading to both mental and physical consequences.

Sleep Disruptions

One of the most common physical manifestations of heartbreak is sleep disturbances. The racing thoughts, anxiety, and emotional pain can make it challenging to fall asleep or stay asleep. This lack of quality rest can leave you exhausted and mentally drained, exacerbating the emotional distress.

Appetite Changes

Heartbreak can affect your appetite in different ways. Some people may lose their appetite and have difficulty eating, leading to weight loss. Others might turn to food for comfort, leading to emotional eating and potential weight gain. These changes in eating habits can further affect your overall well-being.

Weakened Immune System

Prolonged stress and emotional distress can weaken your immune system. You might find yourself more susceptible to illnesses, such as colds or infections. It's essential to prioritize self-care and maintain healthy habits during this vulnerable time.

Aches and Pains

The physical toll of heartbreak can also manifest as physical aches and pains. Many people report feeling tension in their neck, shoulders, and back. This muscle tension is often a physical response to emotional stress and pain.

Gastrointestinal Distress

The gut-brain connection is powerful, and emotional distress can lead to gastrointestinal symptoms. Heartbreak can trigger stomachaches, nausea, and digestive issues. It's common to experience a "knots in the stomach" feeling during this time.

Increased Heart Rate

Heartbreak can lead to an increased heart rate and feelings of palpitations. This physical response results from the body's "fight or flight" response to stress and emotional upheaval.

Headaches

Many individuals going through a breakup report frequent headaches, including tension headaches and migraines. The stress and emotional turmoil can cause blood vessels in the head to constrict and lead to painful headaches.

Coping with the Physical Toll

Understanding that heartbreak can take a physical toll is the first step toward managing it. It's important to practice self-care during this time, including:

Getting Adequate Sleep: Establish a bedtime routine and create a comfortable sleeping environment to improve sleep quality.

Eating Well: Focus on balanced and nutritious meals to provide your body with the energy it needs to cope with stress.

Exercise: Regular physical activity can help reduce stress, release endorphins, and alleviate some physical symptoms of heartbreak.

Mindfulness and Relaxation Techniques: Practices such as meditation, deep breathing, and progressive muscle relaxation can help manage stress and muscle tension.

Seeking Support: Talk to friends, family, or a therapist about your feelings. Sharing your emotions can help reduce stress and the physical toll of heartbreak.

The Impact of Heartbreak on Mental Health

Heartbreak, often stemming from the end of a significant romantic relationship, can have profound effects on a person's mental and physical health. This emotional turmoil can trigger a cascade of responses in the body and mind, leading to both short-term and long-term consequences. Here's a detailed exploration of the impact of heartbreak on mental and physical health:

Emotional Turmoil: Heartbreak can lead to a wide range of intense emotions, including sadness, grief, anger, guilt, and anxiety. These emotions can be overwhelming and persistent, affecting a person's overall mental well-being.

Depression: Prolonged sadness and feelings of hopelessness can develop into clinical depression. Individuals experiencing heartbreak may be at an increased risk of developing depressive symptoms, such as loss of interest in activities, changes in appetite, and sleep disturbances.

Anxiety: The uncertainty and emotional distress of a breakup can trigger anxiety symptoms, including excessive worry, restlessness, and panic attacks. Anxiety can exacerbate the stress associated with heartbreak.

Low Self-Esteem: A breakup can shatter self-esteem, leading to feelings of inadequacy and self-doubt. This can impact self-image and self-worth, which are critical components of mental health.

Isolation: Many individuals going through heartbreak tend to withdraw from social activities and isolate themselves. Social isolation can intensify feelings of loneliness and exacerbate mental health challenges.

Remember that healing from heartbreak is a holistic process that encompasses emotional and physical well-being. By acknowledging and addressing the physical manifestations of heartbreak, you can better care for your body and promote overall healing and recovery.

A breakup is a profoundly personal and emotional journey, and each individual's experience is unique. It's a process marked by a rollercoaster of emotions, from initial shock and sadness to moments of anger, guilt, and acceptance. People often find themselves reflecting on what went wrong, questioning their decisions, and trying to make sense of the sudden void left by the absence of their partner.

The physical and emotional toll of a breakup can be significant, leading to symptoms such as stress, sleep disturbances, changes in appetite, and even physical aches and pains. These manifestations of heartbreak can vary from person to person, as can individuals' coping mechanisms to navigate their healing process.

In this journey, it's important to remember that there's no one-size-fits-all approach to dealing with a breakup. Everyone has their own way of coping, seeking support, and finding closure. However, the need for self-compassion, understanding, and time to heal is universal.

As you go through the heartbreak stages, it's valuable to acknowledge your emotions, seek support from friends and family, and consider professional guidance if needed. Ultimately, a breakup can be a transformative experience, providing an opportunity for personal growth, self-discovery, and the chance to build a stronger, brighter future.

Women's Emotional Responses

Research has shown that women and men often exhibit different emotional responses to breakups. While it's important to note that individual experiences can vary widely, some general trends have been observed. Here are some key emotional responses for women:

Higher Levels of Sadness

Studies have indicated that women tend to experience higher levels of sadness following a breakup. This emotional response can be attributed to women's emotional investment in relationships. As Dr. Jennifer Taitz, a clinical psychologist, explains, "Women tend to be more emotionally expressive and have a greater focus on emotional connection in relationships. This emotional investment can result in deeper feelings of sadness when a relationship ends."

Guilt and Self-Blame

Women sometimes exhibit higher levels of guilt and self-blame after a breakup. Dr. Suzanne Degges-White, a licensed counselor and professor, notes, "Women may be more inclined to internalize relationship problems and blame themselves when things go wrong." This tendency to take on responsibility for the relationship's demise can lead to feelings of guilt and self-doubt.

Need for Emotional Support

Women often seek emotional support from friends, family, or therapists more readily than men. Dr. Kristin Davin, a licensed psychologist, explains, "Women tend to lean on their social networks for emotional support. Sharing their feelings and experiences with others is a common coping mechanism." This support-seeking behavior can be a crucial part of the healing process.

Communication and Processing
Women frequently engage in more active communication and processing of their emotions. According to Dr. Jennifer Kromberg, a licensed psychologist, "Women are often more willing to talk about their feelings and relationship experiences. They may analyze the breakup in-depth and actively seek understanding and closure through communication."

It's important to emphasize that these trends are general observations and do not apply to everyone. Each person's response to a breakup is influenced by various factors, including their personality, upbringing, cultural background, and the circumstances of the relationship's end.

Moreover, the emotional responses to breakups are not limited to one gender, and men, too, can experience sadness, guilt, and a need for emotional support. The gender differences in emotional responses are observed on average but should not be used to stereotype or generalize individual experiences. Each person's journey through a breakup is unique, and understanding and support are crucial regardless of gender.

Men's Emotional Responses

Men's emotional responses to breakups can differ from women's, reflecting unique coping mechanisms and societal expectations. While individual experiences vary widely, here are some key aspects of men's emotional responses to breakups:

Stoicism and Emotional Restraint
Societal norms often condition men to be stoic and emotionally restrained. This can lead them to process their feelings privately and avoid open displays of emotion. Dr. Scott Carol, a psychologist, explains, "Men are frequently raised with the idea that they should be strong and independent. This can result in emotional restraint and a reluctance to express vulnerability."

Distanced Coping Mechanisms
Men sometimes cope with breakups by distancing themselves emotionally. This might involve focusing on work, hobbies, or other distractions to divert their attention from the emotional pain. Dr. Scott Carol notes, "Men often employ distancing strategies to cope. They might throw themselves into work, sports, or other activities to avoid facing their emotions."

Physical Disconnect
Men's bodies can sometimes help them disconnect from the emotional pain. Professor Dawn Maslar, a relationship expert, mentions, "Men may experience a surge in testosterone following a breakup. This hormonal shift can contribute to increased physical energy and a drive to 'move on' from the relationship."

Silent Suffering
Men might silently suffer through a breakup without discussing their feelings with friends or seeking emotional support. Professor Dawn Maslar notes, "Men may be less likely to talk about their feelings or seek therapy after a breakup. They often prefer to suffer in silence, believing it's a sign of strength."

Delayed Emotional Processing
Men may take longer to process their emotions after a breakup, often dealing with them internally and gradually coming to terms with the loss. Dr. Scott Carol adds, "Men may experience a delay in emotional processing. While women might openly express their emotions, men might take time to reflect and make sense of their feelings."

It's important to stress that these observations are general tendencies, not absolutes. Men's emotional responses can vary widely, and many men are comfortable expressing their emotions openly and seeking support during a breakup. The impact of societal expectations on emotional responses is changing, and more men are recognizing the importance of emotional expression and seeking help when needed.

Ultimately, how individuals, regardless of gender, navigate the emotional landscape of a breakup is a deeply personal journey. Understanding and respecting these differences in emotional responses can contribute to more empathetic and supportive relationships during difficult times.

Gender Differences in Processing Breakups

Breaking up is a challenging experience for everyone, but it's essential to recognize that gender differences can influence how individuals navigate the emotional terrain of a breakup. Here's a detailed exploration of these gender differences:

Emotional Bonding

Women often tend to form stronger emotional bonds in relationships. This emotional investment can make breakups particularly painful for women, as they may feel a more profound sense of loss when the relationship ends. This emotional connection can also contribute to a more pronounced sense of sadness and longing.

Emotional Management

Men sometimes struggle with emotional management when dealing with breakups. Societal norms can encourage men to suppress or deal with emotions privately. This can lead to emotional restraint and a reluctance to express vulnerability, making it challenging for some men to openly process their feelings.

Self-Esteem and Vulnerability

The impact of low self-esteem can be significant after a breakup. Both men and women with lower self-esteem may feel more vulnerable and suffer from more significant emotional distress. Low self-esteem can exacerbate feelings of sadness, guilt, and inadequacy.

Expression of Anger and Self-Destructive Behaviors

Men may sometimes express their emotional pain through

anger or self-destructive behaviors. Dr. Jennifer Taitz, a clinical psychologist, said, "Men may be more likely to externalize their pain, engaging in behaviors such as excessive drinking, risk-taking, or impulsive actions as a way to cope with the emotional distress."

Seeking Emotional Support
Women tend to be more open to seeking emotional support from friends, family, or therapists after a breakup. They may actively talk about their feelings and experiences, seeking understanding and closure through communication. This support-seeking behavior is a common coping mechanism for women.

Outward Appearance vs. Internal Struggles
Men often grapple with a disconnect between their outward appearance and internal struggles. They might appear strong and unaffected to the outside world while silently suffering inside. This disparity can sometimes hinder their ability to receive support and understanding from others.

Feelings of Loneliness and Rationalization
Women may experience profound feelings of loneliness after a breakup, which can intensify their emotional responses. To rationalize the end of the relationship, they may replay the events and try to understand what went wrong. This reflective process is part of their emotional healing.

Emotional Response and Recovery
Women often respond faster to a breakup, processing their feelings more immediately and intensely. However, this faster emotional response can also contribute to a quicker recovery, as women may actively seek closure and support to heal.

Hesitance and Rebound Relationships
Women are sometimes more hesitant to enter rebound relationships. They may take more time to heal and process their emotions before seeking new romantic connections. Research

suggests that men are more likely to engage in rebound relationships sooner after a breakup.

It's crucial to emphasize that these gender differences are general trends that may not apply to everyone. Each person's response to a breakup is influenced by various factors, including their personality, upbringing, cultural background, and the specific circumstances of the relationship's end. Understanding and respecting these differences in emotional responses can contribute to more empathetic and supportive relationships during challenging times.

The 7 Stages of Grieving After a Breakup

Desperate for Answers

In the initial aftermath of a breakup, it's common to feel an overwhelming need for answers and explanations. You might replay conversations, events, and decisions, desperately seeking clarity and understanding. The shock of the breakup can leave you grasping for any insight to make sense of the situation. This stage is characterized by an intense urge to find closure and untangle the complex emotions that come with the end of a relationship.

Denial

In the denial stage, individuals often refuse to accept the reality of the breakup. This is a protective mechanism that helps shield you from the immediate pain and emotional upheaval. You may idealize the past and hold onto hope, convincing yourself that the relationship can be restored. Denial allows you to temporarily avoid the full weight of the loss and its associated emotions.

Bargaining

You may engage in a series of "what if" scenarios during the bargaining stage. You might make promises or set conditions for yourself in an attempt to reverse the breakup. This is a manifestation of your desire to regain what has been lost. It's a stage marked by a deep yearning to turn back the clock and make changes that could have prevented the relationship's demise.

Relief
Relief often comes after the initial shock and turmoil of the breakup. As time passes, you may feel a sense of liberation and freedom. The weight of the relationship's challenges begins to lift, and you experience a reduction in emotional pain. It's a stage where you may start to regain a sense of control over your life and well-being.

Anger
Anger is a typical response to heartbreak. In this stage, you may find yourself directing your anger toward various targets, including your ex-partner, yourself, or the situation. It serves as an emotional outlet for the pain and frustration you're experiencing. Anger can be a natural part of the healing process, helping you to externalize your emotions and assert your boundaries.

Depression
Depression is characterized by deep sadness, loneliness, and a profound sense of emptiness. During this stage, you may isolate yourself from others, lose interest in activities you once enjoyed, and struggle with daily routines. It's a time when the emotional weight of the breakup can be overwhelming, leading to a sense of despair and hopelessness.

Acceptance
Acceptance is the final stage in the grieving process. It's the point where you come to terms with the reality of the breakup. While you may not forget the relationship, you can acknowledge that it is now a part of your past. This stage marks a pivotal moment of moving forward, focusing on personal growth, and being open to new opportunities and connections. Acceptance is about finding closure and embracing the potential for a brighter future.

Attachment Styles and Their Importance in Self-Awareness

Attachment styles are pivotal in shaping an individual's approach to relationships and self-awareness. These styles are developed in early childhood and continue to influence adult relationships. Understanding your attachment style can provide insights into your emotional needs, relationship behaviors, and self-awareness.

If you are unfamiliar with attachment styles, I wanted to introduce them because they may have played a role in the relationship. As someone myself who has identified with an anxious attachment style, this can make a breakup even more difficult because your biggest fear is abandonment. The good news is that attachment styles are changeable but take work. Here is a little more information on attachment styles so that you can better understand yourself or your past partners and shed more light on things that went wrong.

Secure Attachment Style
Individuals with a secure attachment style have a positive view of themselves and others. They are comfortable with both intimacy and independence, seeking emotional support and providing it to their partners. They are confident in their relationships, characterized by trust and mutual support.

Understanding a secure attachment style can boost self-awareness by reinforcing one's ability to establish and maintain healthy, fulfilling relationships. Secure individuals are more in tune with their emotional needs and can navigate conflicts and challenges effectively.

Preoccupied (Anxious) Attachment Style
People with a preoccupied attachment style, also known as anxious attachment, often seek high levels of closeness and

approval from their partners but may doubt their worthiness of love. They are often preoccupied with their relationships and fear rejection or abandonment. This attachment style can lead to emotional highs and lows and a desire for constant reassurance.

Recognizing a preoccupied attachment style can enhance self-awareness by shedding light on seeking external validation and reassurance patterns. It can prompt self-reflection on underlying insecurities and how they impact relationships.

If you may also relate to an anxious attachment style, I have a book covering the ins and outs of anxious attachment that guides you to adopt a more secure attachment style. You can find this book on Amazon called "Free Yourself from Anxious Attachment."

Fearful (Avoidant) Attachment Style
Fearful or avoidant individuals often want emotional closeness but are hesitant to engage in relationships fully. They fear getting hurt, often due to past relationship experiences, and can be emotionally distant or guarded. A push-pull dynamic characterizes this attachment style.

Acknowledging a fearful attachment style can deepen self-awareness by highlighting an inner conflict between the desire for intimacy and a fear of vulnerability. Understanding this style can prompt individuals to explore past traumas or relationship experiences contributing to their emotional patterns.

The Connection Between Attachment Styles and Adult Relationships
Attachment styles established in childhood can significantly influence adult relationships. Those with a secure attachment style tend to form healthier and more stable relationships marked by trust and communication. However, individuals with anxious attachment styles may struggle with constant relationship worries, while those with fearful styles may experience difficulty with emotional intimacy and maintaining long-term relationships.

Recognizing your attachment style is a powerful tool for self-awareness. It allows you to understand your emotional needs, your relationship reactions, and areas where personal growth and healing may be necessary. It can also help you make more informed choices in selecting partners and navigating the complexities of adult relationships. Self-awareness regarding your attachment style empowers you to work on developing healthier patterns and fostering more fulfilling connections with others.

Assessing and Processing Emotions Worksheet

Emotional self-awareness is a crucial step in healing after a breakup. Use this worksheet to identify and manage your emotions, referencing the feelings you may experience following a breakup. An example is provided for clarity.

Step 1. Identifying Your Emotions

Take a moment to reflect on your emotions. You may experience a mix of feelings after a breakup.
Check the emotions you're currently feeling or write down any additional ones:

Sadness _____   Anger _____

Guilt _____   Loneliness _____

Fear _____   Relief _____

Confusion _____   Regret _____

Frustration _____   Resentment _____

Acceptance ____   Empowerment _____

Hope _____   Other _____

Step 2. Rating Your Emotions

On a scale of 1 to 10, with 1 being mild and 10 being intense, rate the intensity of each emotion you selected in Step 1:

Sadness: _____   Anger: _____   Guilt: _____

Loneliness: _____   Fear: _____   Relief: _____

Confusion: _____   Regret: _____   Frustration: _____

Resentment: _____   Acceptance: _____ Hope: _____

Empowerment: _____ Other _____

Step 3. Recognizing Triggers

Identify any specific triggers or situations that intensify or alleviate your emotions.

For example, think about what makes you feel sadder or more hopeful. This can provide insight into how to manage your emotions effectively.

Trigger 1:

Trigger 2:

Trigger 3:

Step 4. Strategies for Managing Emotions

Based on the emotions you've identified and their intensity, list strategies that may help you healthily manage these emotions. Consider coping mechanisms such as talking to a friend, practicing mindfulness, journaling, or seeking professional help.

Strategy 1:

Strategy 2:

Strategy 3:

Remember that processing and managing your emotions is a personal journey, and it's okay to seek help when needed. Use this worksheet as a tool to guide your self-awareness and emotional healing after a breakup.

2

Emotional Responses After A Breakup

When a relationship ends, emotions can run high, and the digital world often becomes a battleground for heartbroken individuals. Instead of just moving on, many of us engage in what could be described as "digital warfare." It's when we block, unfriend, or even secretly watch our ex-partner's online activities. Have you ever wondered why we resort to such actions? What are the natural consequences of publicly shaming an ex on social media?

Consider this story: Someone on my friends list publicly posted out of anger that his ex gave him an STD. The worst part about it is the person he was posting about was the mother of his child. Now, even though these people were more acquaintances to me, it just really stuck in my memory of how awful it is to share information like that in public. In this chapter, we explore the impulsive and sometimes regrettable actions that often follow a breakup in the digital age and their impact on our journey to healing from heartbreak.

Keep Personal Matters Private: Remember that social media can be perceived as a place to let go of steam; however, information remains online permanently when posted. Think twice before posting.

Avoid Sub-tweeting or Vague Posting: Such posts usually confuse and create contradictions. It is advisable to communicate with the person directly.

Remember Your Audience: They are family, children, friends, workmates, or employers who follow you. Remember that you're always displaying your image online.

Seek Support Offline: Instead of turning to social media, lean on close friends, family, or professionals who can offer guidance and a listening ear.

Social Media Post-Split

The Digital Detox: Unfollowing Your Ex
While it's true that every relationship and its aftermath are unique, there's a universal truth: space is essential. If your relationship ends on good terms and you want to remain friends, you may not need to cut ties with your ex. Nonetheless, contemplate the perks of muting or concealing their updates. It will mean that you don't keep on remembering them and get the free mind to heal. You must understand that it's not about cutting them from your life but creating space for your healing.

Resisting the Urge: Avoiding Their Profile
Digital curiosity is a natural human trait. But when it comes to checking out your ex's page, it's essential to ask yourself: The answer to "What will this achieve?" is usually more pain or confusion. Rather than looking for coded messages and updates about your healing, commit to your healing.

Tips for a Healthy Digital Post-Breakup

Your Journey vs. Theirs: Remember, everyone heals differently. Do not compare your singlehood journey with that of your ex-lover.

Obsession is Natural But temporary: it's all right to be obsessed first. Acknowledge it and move on from that.

Prioritize Your Mental Health: If your mental health is at stake because of your ex's online persona, consider shutting them out.

Mute Mutual Friends: It can be wise to mute them for a while if they continuously post about your ex.

Erase Triggers: Remove posts that may generate painful reminiscences.

Stay Discreet: Avoid posting about the breakup. Your healing journey is personal.

Self-Care is Key: Focus on posting about your growth, achievements, and happiness.

Kyra Kyles, former Editor in Chief at Ebony magazine, once wisely said,

"When freshly broken up, distance is key."

This sentiment is crucial in the digital age. While it might seem challenging, I always remember the words of my dear friend Ammie, "If it's hurting you, stop doing it."

When Blocking Becomes Essential

It's not about grudges and hostility; it is about saving oneself. This is where you realize that your ex's activities on social networks are hampering your healing process. Indeed, as Robert, a writer from Nebraska, succinctly stated, "Do not just unfriend them. Particularly when you believe you can be a mere 'tourist' in their life whenever you find time to access social media.

Family and Friends: The Extended Digital Web

It is tricky when it comes to your ex's family and friends. Suppose it does not affect your posts. Why bother? But if they are going to act as sources of pain, then muting or unfollowing is a good option. Remember, your well-being comes first.

Posting with Purpose

You may be compelled to engage in cathartic posting on social media occasionally. However, ensure whatever you wish to post at any time is intentional. Do not post impulsively, as you might live to regret such posts. So, link, mend, and develop using social media. Shana says, "Follow those accounts that make you laugh and connect with others."

The take-home message is that every tweet, click, and post you make on social media after breaking up should help you heal and recover. It is a journey, and while the digital era is increasingly complicated, it also provides tools for communion, meditation, and love of oneself.

The "Relationship Status" Transition

The "Relationship Status" feature in a social media world where everything is a statement to the world has its significance. It is not like a status, but a digital statement about love life. So, when a relationship concludes, the question arises: At what point should they change this status?

An Emotional Weight of a Digital Status: Sharing your relationship status publicly on some platforms, for instance, Facebook or another platform, could be exciting for you, too. Such an evolution from single to in a relationship can be very fulfilling. Life seldom comes as easy as that. Some people choose to set their default Facebook status as "It's Complicated" when a relationship becomes complicated. The unstable, volatile relationship of the digital age reflects this status.

The Subtlety of Status Transition: Rather than making such drastic changes, being discreet by hiding relationship status or privacy settings can be a more sympathetic measure. This approach serves multiple purposes:

Time for Healing: It takes time to make a final break up with your partner, and therefore, you give yourself and your former partner some breathing space by not announcing the break immediately. This is very emotional, so this subtlety enables you to handle the situation without the additional pressure of society knowing.

Reduced Scrutiny: A social media break after a breakup is typical. To mitigate the immediacy of the breakup, you can opt to hide your relationship status if you want during this break. This helps since by the time you return and decide to change it, the immediacy of the breakup will have diminished. The event is quickly turned into 'old news,' reducing the chances of friends and acquaintances prying on the details.

Consideration for Your Ex: Acknowledging your ex-partner by not updating your status immediately is a nice gesture. Such a change could be immediately seen as hasty and heartless, only aggravating emotional troubles.

Post Breakup: Understanding the Impact.

In the first place, it is essential to acknowledge that a relationship breakdown can be very emotionally damaging. Dr. Winch is a licensed psychologist, renowned speaker, and author. According to him, these post-breakup feelings are similar to desperation because they emerge due to the uncontrollable wish for a reunion. Such emotional turmoil could result in behaviors contrary to a person's personality. For example, one could be perpetually calling an ex or be visibly distraught at work. The first stage involves recognizing and accepting how one feels.

Find Closure in Your Terms: Breakups can be troublesome if they occur without warning or during other challenging moments in life. According to Dr. Winch, closure can only be achieved individually. The person will gradually occupy less mental space once you emotionally detains. Think of the difficulties of the relationship and how they can enable you to view the issues more objectively and allow your healing.

Discover Yourself: Every end brings a new beginning. Reconnect with yourself during this transition. Learn how to meet your emotional needs, practice thankfulness, and cultivate habits conducive to your objectives. Making the shift from 'us' to 'me' in the healing process is quite essential.

Leverage Work as a Constructive Distraction: However, it becomes hard to resist having a prolonged vacation; work may be an excellent diversion to healing. Participate in activities you love and undertake projects that make you feel accomplished.

Hold On to Hope: Healing through seeing and visualizing a brighter future. Picture when the soreness disappears, and you come out of it better. Recall previous hardships and remind yourself that if you have managed to deal with difficulties, you can overcome them this time.

Dr. Winch's perspectives turned out to be immensely useful in my journey. By diving into the fulfilling activities and deep thought, I regained my identity apart from the relationship. Journaling became a therapeutic outlet whereby I could plot my healing process and set future goals.

Psychological Resolution: Breakups are challenging, and sharing mutual friends with your ex adds another layer of complexity. Over two decades of analyzing relationships, I've seen countless individuals grapple with this situation. Here's a guide on handling mutual friendships post-breakup with grace, understanding, and maturity.

Maintain Respect for Everyone Involved: Avoid speaking negatively about your ex, even if hurt or angry. Remember, your friends care about both of you, and it's unfair to put them in a position where they feel they have to defend or choose sides. Don't be mean to your previous love out in the open, though you can tell them how low you feel inside to someone you can trust. You should also find a friend or family member who will listen but will not spread it because that would be bad news for you. It could serve as therapy for you and show respect to others involved.

Steer Clear of Drama: It's essential not to involve your mutual friends in any disputes or disagreements you might have with your ex. They shouldn't be placed in the middle of your matters.

Communicate Your Needs Clearly: Your friends might be treading lightly, unsure what to say or do. Open up a dialogue. Let them know your boundaries regarding discussing your ex or attending the same events. By setting clear expectations, you make it easier for everyone.

Embrace Change with an Open Heart: Relationships evolve, and some friendships might shift or drift after a breakup. While it's painful, it's also a natural part of life. Cherish the memories and focus on the friends who remain steadfast. I always try to look for the positives and think well, there is something better waiting for me shortly.

Seek Joyful Moments: Spend quality time with your mutual friends. Engage in activities that uplift your spirits, whether trying out a new hobby or revisiting old favorites. This is a time for healing and rediscovery.

Prioritize Openness: If friends have questions or concerns, address them with honesty. Avoid laying blame or delving into the nitty-gritty details of the breakup. Stick to the facts and express your feelings without casting aspersions.

Share Time Equitably: Understand that your friends want to spend time with you and your ex. Propose alternating weeks or events to ensure everyone gets their fair share of time without awkward encounters.

Choose Friendships Wisely: Reflect on which friendships genuinely enrich your life. Not all mutual friends will be an excellent fit post-breakup. Focus on those who support and uplift you.

Stay Graceful in Shared Spaces: There will be times when you and your ex are in the same space. In such instances, remain courteous and avoid confrontations. If tensions rise, it's always best to exit gracefully.

Avoid Possessiveness: It's natural to feel protective of your friends but avoid the urge to "claim" them. Friendships aren't about ownership. Let friends gravitate naturally, and remember that genuine friendships will withstand the test of time.

Coping with Judgment after a Breakup

Post-breakup, you might face judgment or unsolicited advice from others.

Stay Confident: Understand your worth. Don't let others' opinions define your self-worth or decisions.

Limit Exposure: If specific individuals are consistently judgmental, limit your interactions with them.

Seek Support: Surround yourself with supportive friends and family. They can offer a counter-narrative to the judgment you might be facing.

Educate and Inform: Sometimes, judgment stems from ignorance. If you feel comfortable, educate the person about your reasons without getting defensive.

Professional Help

If the judgment affects your mental well-being, consider seeking therapy or counseling. Professionals can provide coping strategies and a safe space to express your feelings.

Loneliness and Its Impact on Mental Health

Loneliness is more than just a fleeting emotion; it's a complex state of mind that can profoundly affect one's mental well-being. Over the past two decades, I've observed and studied the intricate relationship between loneliness and various mental health issues. Here's a comprehensive look at the interplay between loneliness, depression, anxiety, and the risk of suicide.

The Link Between Loneliness and Depression

Loneliness can indeed be a precursor to depression. When individuals feel isolated and disconnected, they may experience overwhelming sadness, hopelessness, and a sense of worthlessness. These feelings can intensify over time, leading to clinical depression. Conversely, those already suffering from depression might isolate themselves from social interactions, further deepening their sense of loneliness.

Loneliness and Its Connection to Suicide

The correlation between loneliness and suicide is particularly concerning. Loneliness can impress feelings of despair, making one feel as though they're trapped in their isolation with no way out. Especially among the youth, where the need for social connection is paramount, loneliness can amplify suicidal ideation. These feelings can escalate Without proper support and intervention, posing a severe risk.

The Interplay of Anxiety and Loneliness

Anxiety, with its excessive worry and fear, can be both a cause and a result of loneliness. Individuals who feel lonely might develop social anxiety, fearing judgment or rejection in social settings. This fear can deter them from seeking social interactions, further entrenching their feelings of isolation. On the flip side, those with preexisting anxiety disorders might find it challenging to engage in social situations, leading to increased feelings of loneliness.

Dividing Finances and Belongings after Separation
Whether you are going through a divorce or just a long-term relationship breakup, it is a painful process in its own right, and the division of assets only complicates matters. Here's a comprehensive guide to help you handle this complex situation:

If Your Ex-Partner Managed the Finances

The process of untangling finances after a breakup can be incredibly challenging. It often involves splitting shared assets and debts and deciding who keeps what, leading to heated disagreements and resentment. Moreover, if one person was the primary breadwinner or had more control over the finances, the other person may feel vulnerable and uncertain about their financial future. This can lead to feelings of economic instability and anxiety, adding an extra layer of stress to an already emotionally charged situation.

To navigate this difficult period, open and honest communication is essential. Both parties should be willing to discuss their financial situation calmly and rationally to reach a fair and mutually agreeable resolution. Seeking the guidance of a mediator or financial advisor can also be beneficial in helping to divide assets and debts equitably. While the emotional pain of a breakup may take time to heal, addressing the financial aspects with care and respect can provide a sense of closure and help both individuals move forward on solid ground, ready to embrace a new chapter in their lives.

Agreeing on Finances: First, make a list of assets and liabilities. This encompasses real estate, money, home equipment, and the vehicle. If you need more clarification about the value of your possessions, consult experts.

Decide on the method of distribution of properties and expenses incurred. In case there is a dispute, consult with a mediator or lawyer. Discuss your financial support for the children, if any. Usually, both parents are expected to contribute. It is essential to document the financial agreement because it will prevent future conflicts after the marriage fails.

Home and Pension Division

Buying Out Your Ex-Partner: If you intend to keep the house, one option is to buy out your ex. Nonetheless, the mortgage lender will require proof that you can meet the payment obligations independently. This is usually a challenge for people who are not working or working part-time. Can you go over to interest only? Mortgage, if the regular repayments are beyond control. Talk with your financial consultant before making any decision.

Selling Your Home: Discuss with your ex-partner if selling is the best option. If the home is highly appreciated, living together is better; however, if there is little equity, only one should remain in it. The balance left to pay is known as equity. Hence, for example, if a house sells at $400,000 but has a mortgage of $200,000, the equity is $200,000. Do not forget that the totals will likely be reduced due to realtor fees and other home-selling expenses. A professional should also be involved in explaining the splitting of equity. Several property valuations must also be obtained.

Dividing Your Pension: You may claim part of your former partner's pension if you are married or in a civil partnership. One must also talk and come to a consensus on handling the pension. It is advisable to consult with a financial adviser.

Pension sharing is the most usual approach, in which part of the pension is shifted to the other partner's fund. This calls for an "order of pension sharing," a legal term.

Worksheet: Evaluating the Need to Block Your Ex

Post-breakup dynamics can be challenging. One of the most debated decisions is whether to block an ex-partner from your life, especially on social media. This worksheet aims to help you assess your feelings and circumstances to make an informed choice.

Should You Block Your Ex? A Self-Assessment

Please answer the following questions honestly:

1. Does your ex frequently attempt to communicate with you online?

[   ] Yes

[   ] No

2. Have you noticed your ex excessively engaging with your online activities, such as liking multiple photos or posts quickly?

[   ] Yes

[   ] No

3. Do you find it hard to resist the urge to check your ex's online profiles or activities?

[   ] Yes

[   ] No

4. Does the thought of your ex viewing your online activities make you uncomfortable?

[   ] Yes

[   ] No

5. Do you feel that seeing your ex's online activities hinders your healing process?

[   ] Yes

[   ] No

If you've answered 'Yes' to 3 or more of the above questions, it might benefit your emotional well-being to consider blocking your ex. Blocking can provide the mental space you need to heal and move forward without constant reminders or potential intrusions from your past relationship.

Reflecting on the Decision to Unblock Your Ex

If you've decided to block your ex, it's essential to know when, or if, it's appropriate to reverse that decision. Before unblocking, ponder on the following:

1. Personal Growth: Have you genuinely moved past the relationship?

2. New Relationships: Are you involved with someone new, and is the relationship stable?

3. Forgiveness: Have you genuinely forgiven your ex for past grievances?

4. Online Behavior: Has your ex respected your boundaries and stopped intrusive online behaviors?

5. Emotional vestiges: Do you still harbor romantic feelings for your ex?

Throughout this chapter, we've delved deep into the intricacies of handling post-breakup dynamics. We've explored the emotional rollercoaster that ensues, the importance of supportive communities, and the delicate decision to block an ex from one's life. Each section was designed to provide you with actionable insights and tools to make informed choices that prioritize your emotional well-being.

As we close this chapter, it's essential to recognize that while understanding and managing the immediate aftermath of a breakup is crucial, the journey doesn't end there. Healing is a process requiring time, patience, and the right strategies.

Coming Up - Coping and Healing

The next chapter, "Coping and Healing," promises to be a beacon of hope and a guide for those traversing the challenging path of recovery. We'll delve into the heart of the healing journey, ensuring you're equipped with the knowledge and tools to move forward with resilience and grace.

You'll learn how to

- Handle the complexities of the healing process.

- Effectively manage overwhelming emotions that threaten to derail your progress.

- Incorporate mindfulness practices to stay present and grounded.

- Establish and maintain healthy boundaries, ensuring you

protect your peace.

- Harness the power of journaling and meditation, two proven tools that can significantly aid recovery.

The healing journey is unique for everyone, but with the proper guidance, you can transform this challenging period into a time of growth and self-discovery. So, please take a deep breath and embark on this transformative journey together.

3
Coping and Healing

Understanding your emotional response to a breakup can help you feel less alone...

There comes a point in your relationship that you do not want to believe that your relationship with your loved one is ending. It is hard to believe, yet challenging to cope with and handle yourself in tough scenarios. While you accept that your relationship was awful, it was even unbearable at times; the thought of living without it is unacceptable. However, moving on while living the life you never imagined would be best. When you realize that you two can't make it, you start to understand that it is happening; yes, it is finally over. You have gone from "Don't leave me" to "Okay, I am giving up."

You now feel nothing but only being "okay." However, your memories will chase you daily, like waiting for your ex's calls and hoping your phone will pop up with their notification. This is when you will gradually realize that you have left each other's space, and the reality of losing your relationship hits you. Understandably, the process is brutal, and it requires a long time to feel loved again until your mind starts processing again, till you become independent in your emotions and plan to reshape your life path.

During your relationship, when things were not going the way you wanted, when your relationship with your ex started suffering, this was the moment you might have realized that a breakup was coming. While you knew things were not going well for months or even years, you were still blindsided. But now the breakup is happening, you might be overwhelmed and haunted by the loss of fear without this person.

To help you anticipate your breakup journey, here are some stages you can relate to and support yourself in letting go.

Desperate for Answers
The drive to know about everything is consuming and comes from rational overthinking and rational behaviors. Therefore, instead of overthinking, you should understand why this happened and how it benefited your mental and physical health.

You fixate on things your ex said in both angry and happy conditions. There will also be a time when you start blaming yourself for the cause of the breakup. But, sometimes, you have moments of clarity, too, when you discover the magnitude of your loss and finally accept it's over.

I remember in a past relationship where I was unhappy, and I wanted the relationship to be over, but when it was finally over, I felt so lost. I had a fear of the future and a fear of being alone. Not only was I losing a partner, but I also had to change my life completely. At that time, I was living with my partner, so I had to start looking for a new place to move to. It was such a challenging time.

Your daily life's pain, confusion, and disorganization can become all you keep thinking and talking about. But it would be best to remain confident that this breakup has happened for a reason and that something better awaits you at the end of the tunnel. However, the desire to understand something so desperately forces you to debate with family, friends, colleagues, and even strangers about the ending of your relationship. You give them reasons with justifications.

Denial

Often at night, you wake up from horrible dreams and think it can't be true why it is happening. You may feel incomplete without your ex as you have put every little effort to keep the relationship going. After all, that relationship was all your world and your life, so it's hard to believe it is over.

To save your relationship, you funnel every hope, even if it costs you well-being. You postpone your needs to grieve the relationship ending because it is just too painful to face. You hinder the grieving process by replacing it with unrealistic hopes that your relationship can still be recovered.

Bargaining

The worst thing after breakups happen is your will to avoid acceptance that your relationship has ended. Your thoughts start killing you in the form of overthinking like I could be a better and more attentive partner; I should not have done this to make my partner angry; I can never be a good person to be involved in relationships again. You will try to make your pain go away by winning your ex back at any cost.

But wait, ask yourself, is this a logical thing you are doing now? You need to understand that you are on the edge of what feels like an abyss and try hard not to fall into the unknown and self-imaginary traps. You can hope for new good things to happen in the coming life but never expect expectations to prevent you from losing, which can put you in a better position.

However, during this phase of the healing journey, you must promise that you will fix all your problems at all costs. You will sometimes find yourself alone to repair and maintain your life, but this is how only you can help you work.

Try your hardest to accept that the relationship ended because of the contributions of both parties. You cannot take responsibility for every damage; somewhere deep inside, you already know that.

Bargaining can be distracted after facing a loss. Reality comes crashing down again and again. Moreover, when you bargain, you try to take responsibility for why the relationship didn't work, which may give you the illusion that you have control over it.

Relapse

Breakup pain is always intolerable, and you might try to convince your ex to try again. You will temporarily relieve the sufferings of withdrawal. However, you can't carry the relationship solo despite your best efforts because it will not end well. Unfortunately, you might need to go through the reconciliation phase more than once before you are convinced it is time to let go.

Sometimes, when people break up with someone they were in a relationship with, they might feel unfortunate and want to get back together with that person. This can make them feel better for a little while. But if only one person tries fixing the relationship, it usually doesn't work out in the end. So, some people might break up and then get back together with the same person more than once before finally deciding to move on for good.

Anger

With a breakup, you experience different feelings; one of them is anger. Breaking up drops you into the unknown, which can call up immobilizing fear and dread. Therefore, when you feel angry, it is because you are letting go of fear, which you have no control over.

When you manage to access anger, the experience becomes empowering because there are shades of remembering your matter, too. You realize that you deserve more from a relationship. Your anger depends on certain temperament, family, and life experiences.

No matter the cause of your anger, it is meant to empower you. Accessing your anger can provide you with the right direction and a feeling of aliveness that becomes numb by loss. It makes you feel that you deserve more.

Even the most crippling and self-defeating anger towards oneself can be considered a natural component of the grieving process. It indicates that you are processing the loss since you are moving through the mourning process. It suggests that you are, somewhere, causing yourself enough internal agony to help you adjust your perception of how the relationship has been. It may force you to take the initiative and make changes if you are willing.

Acceptance
This kind of acceptance happens in the early stage of the process, which feels more like surrender to you. You are still holding up the break yourself because you have to, not because you want to. Maybe your ex or you have concluded that you guys are not meant to be. Over time, this initial stage becomes more substantive because both of you recognize that no boundaries should be respected. Ultimately, you grasp that it is not suitable for you to keep trying anymore.

Redirected Hope
In any relationship, the feeling that keeps us connected is "hope." When hope shatters, it not only makes things to let go but also makes our journey of moving on challenging. But when you accept the reality and start moving forward, you singlehandedly save your relations to the possibility that you can survive without your ex.

It's jarring when you are forced to redirect yourself from the known entity into the chasm of the unknown. However, you can turn your life force into hope in this breakup phase.

The stages of sorrow that accompany any event, including breakups, can occur in minutes or even seconds, over days, months, or years, and then abruptly flip around, leaving you feeling, especially at first, completely unsupported. You have a sense of isolation or alienation from yourself. But moving on in life requires learning to live without that aspect of yourself and coming up with strategies to make up for its loss, just like with any emotional amputation.

Moreover, it is crucial to recognize that there is a method to sort out things for a chaotic grieving process. Know that you are not alone in the grieving process; millions are in the same boat as you. Your condition is a collective and relatable for many people worldwide. Without it, we would not be able to understand different phases of life and how to handle pains and losses in our lives.

As you progress in your process, you will start to see ways through to a point where you can let go of your self-protective course. This is a way to take it as the new beginning of your new life ahead.

Setting the Stage for Healing

Your relationship is over, and you finally have deleted all memories together from everywhere, be it social media, photo frames, or pictures kept in a phone gallery. You feel yourself alone, and it sucks. No matter how much you try to keep yourself busy, meeting friends, listening to songs, and enjoying your favorite activity or hobby, at the end of the day, when you lie in your bed, all the memories will surely hit you. You will want to run away from them; nothing is in your control. In short, you feel that your pain does not seem to get better.

The journey of thought will hit you like a storm, and you will get negative thoughts about not finding love again. It is time to bring some positive change in life, but how?

With the help of mindful self-compassion, you can heal your soul after a breakup. Let's learn mindful self-compassion and how to get help from it.

What is Mindful Self-Compassion?

It refers to treating and loving yourself and the people you love. It is a reality that sometimes people like to keep others happy. They treat people better and help them think positively in life. However, when it comes to them, they are pessimistic about themselves. Remember, you carry the same heart as others; it depends on how you treat it.

It is essential to note that self-compassion is all about loving and making yourself strong. Mindful self-compassion is not about feeling sorry and pity for yourself for what you have not done. It is now time to show yourself some love with happiness.

Think about what you do in your daily routine or a week for your kids, parents, work, friends, and the person who broke your heart. Keep those thoughts aside and consider what you do for yourself. You will realize you give yourself less importance than you bless others.

Our broken heart deserves to be treated well and filled with happiness. You must take some time out for yourself and be nice to it. But you might think about how it would help and how mindful self-compassion can mend your broken heart.

Understanding mindful self-compassion and applying it in your life are two different things. According to research by scientists, there are four steps to turn philosophy into practice.

Step 1 - Accept that You Have Broken Up
After a breakup, many people don't express their feelings. In short, they resist the truth. It is a universal fact that you defy your healing process when you fight the truth with a broken heart.

Acknowledge your pain and accept that your pain came from a failed relationship. If you feel like crying, cry your heart out and help your heart relieve pain through tears. Once you have acknowledged the pain, you can address it very clearly.

Step 2 - Take it as a Rough Phase of Life
You will not feel alone when you understand that many people are in the same boat and going through a challenging phase of their lives.

Heartbreak is a normal part of life; many people experience it differently. Your heartbreak is real but temporary, and it's just a human moment. Everybody experiences it once in their life. When you see people in your surroundings going through the same situation, you will realize you are not the only victim and don't need to feel sorry for yourself.

Step 3 - Be Kind With Yourself
When you go through the breakup process, you will have mixed feelings, such as feelings of anger, anxiety, frustration, and irritation. Due to this reason, you neglect your heart by stopping listening to it. You always feel angry and don't feel like talking and sharing your feelings with everyone because you think nobody will ever understand you. However, leave people aside and try to comprehend your emotions and ways to tackle them.

When you are kind to yourself, you recognize that no one was ever kind to you and your feelings, even the person who broke your heart.

Step 4 - Determine the Ways to be Kind to Yourself
When you find ways to be kind to yourself, you will see the world differently. But how will you do it?

Promise yourself to be patient and allow yourself to try new life experiences or will love your appearance. When you focus on your goal, you can quickly adapt to that lifestyle.

Identify Your Needs

With a broken heart, you might miss the person who broke your heart. You will want him to return as you were used to him. At this point, you need to differentiate between your attachment and love for that person. Your love for your ex will gradually fade when you lose passion. It's all a matter of time!

You Crave for Love

After a breakup, when you begin to feel lonely, you're often overwhelmed by countless thoughts. You might ask yourself if you met that person only to lose them. You start missing them, and believing you're genuinely yearning for love becomes challenging. It's essential to realize that it's not just "love," and you can find it in other places or within yourself.

During this challenging phase, give yourself the love and attention you deserve. List the things you want the perfect partner to do for you and do for yourself. Lastly, pay attention to your intuitions. Listen, treat, and compliment yourself.

Pros of Mindful Self-Compassion

There are plentiful benefits of mindful self-compassion. It eases your heartbreak for feeling happy. When you suffer heartbreak, your subconscious mind tells you that you will never find happiness again. However, by practicing mindful self-compassion, you will re-live your life and smile again. You will become more optimistic about the future. You may start believing in love again and consider yourself powerful for facing any future situations. Slowly, you will recognize you do not need anything to make yourself feel good. This way, you can help yourself prevent future pain from affecting you as much.

Once you start loving yourself, you glow differently. This is very attractive because other people will want to love you, too. When you are ready for a new relationship, it will be easier for you to keep it, and it might last, too.

Don't Undervalue Your Powerful Mind

You are vital, and heartbreak can never break you. It may affect you, but your powerful mind will control your emotions in the healing process. It's time to take some steps by loving yourself. Many people put themselves at the bottom of the to-do list. If you are a victim of heartbreak, you need to place your name first in the list for being new. Trust me, everyone will appreciate the new you.

Dealing with Your Emotions After a Breakup

After a breakup, it's common to experience various emotions, including sadness and anger. However, one emotion that might catch you by surprise is anxiety. You might wonder, "Why am I anxious when the relationship ends?"

Anxiety, in the context of a breakup, can manifest as more than worry. It often becomes a part of the post-breakup distress experience. You may find yourself constantly replaying the events of your past relationship and the breakup, unable to escape these thoughts.

The good news is that these feelings won't last forever. There are effective strategies to help you navigate through post-breakup anxiety, and we're here to provide you with eight of them.

Spend Quality Time with Yourself

Feeling lost after a breakup is natural because romantic relationships can significantly influence your identity and sense of self. The end of a relationship leaves a void where love and connection used to reside, which can trigger pain, stress, and anxiety.

When feeling alone and hurt, the immediate instinct may be to seek comfort from someone else – a friend, family member, or even a rebound partner. There's nothing wrong with seeking support, but setting aside some time for self-discovery is essential. This can help ease anxious feelings and kickstart your healing journey. To begin rebuilding your connection with yourself:

Reflect on Your Relationship and Breakup Experience
Contemplate how your past relationship and breakup have provided valuable insights into your needs and self-awareness. What have you learned about yourself through these experiences? How can you apply this newfound understanding to create more robust and fulfilling relationships in the future?

Pause Before Jumping into a New Relationship
It's essential to pause and reflect before actively pursuing a new relationship. Rushing into a new connection before fully processing your feelings about your previous partner can hinder your personal growth and healing. Any unresolved anxiety and fears from the past may resurface when you engage with a new partner.

Take Inventory of Your Habits and Beliefs
Analyze any new habits and beliefs developed during your previous relationship. Are these changes a true reflection of your desires, interests, and values? Or did you adopt these traits solely to strengthen your connection with your ex-partner?

Incorporate Mindfulness into Your Daily Routine
While mindfulness isn't a magical solution, making an effort to live more mindfully can significantly assist in managing day-to-day anxiety and overall distress.

Dealing with Emotions After Breakups

When you're going through emotional disruption, like anxiety, your instinct may urge you to avoid and suppress the pain, hoping it will disappear on its own. However, avoiding your emotions is not a sustainable coping strategy. The feelings you push aside often grow more substantial and overwhelming, making them challenging to handle independently.

Naming and facing these emotions may initially seem challenging, but it's a crucial step. Over time, you'll find it easier to recognize and release these complicated feelings before they negatively impact your well-being.

Mindfulness practices can be beneficial in this process. They enhance your awareness of your thoughts and emotions, allowing you to stay present in the moment instead of getting consumed by anxiety and worry. Living mindfully involves appreciating everyday experiences and your loved ones and taking the time to savor life's small pleasures.

Maintain a Balanced Perspective

Breakups can be incredibly painful, especially if you don't want the relationship to end in the first place. If your partner initiates the breakup, thoughts of it can intensify feelings of abandonment and rejection. This can trigger a cycle of intrusive thoughts and overthinking that disrupts your daily life.

Rejection can also lead to self-doubt. Taking all the blame for the relationship's end and unquestioningly accepting any "flaws" your ex pointed out can harm your self-esteem and self-confidence.

Blaming your ex entirely might seem like a quick way to move on, but research indicates it can leave you holding onto negative emotions. Instead, adopting a more balanced perspective can lead to a smoother path to healing.

Breakups often result from a combination of factors. So, regardless of who initiated the breakup, both of you played a role. Acknowledging your contributions and considering external and situational factors can help you view the separation more objectively and facilitate the healing process.

Prioritize Self-Care
Self-care is always crucial for maintaining your health and well-being. It becomes even more essential when you're dealing with stress, anxiety, and other forms of distress.

Embrace Your Favorite Activities
You suddenly find yourself with more free time on your hands after break up. This newfound freedom can be a gift, but it can also feel like an eternity when you're grappling with the aftermath of the relationship's end. Those empty hours can become a breeding ground for dwelling on the past, frustrations, uncertainties, and grief.

Engaging in activities you enjoy can be a lifesaver during this time, providing positive distractions throughout the day. It's perfectly fine to divert your mind from unwelcome thoughts if you don't ignore your emotions entirely. Since anxiety can make it challenging to focus, opt for relaxing hobbies to help you during moments when it's hard to concentrate.

Watch a favorite comedy, get lost in a good book, or stroll through your cherished park. The key is to select something simple that brings you joy.

Spend Time with Your Loved Ones
Breakups can cause shame or remorse, mainly if your friends and family still think highly of your ex. It can be challenging to explain the split, and you might not want to relive the hurt your ex-partner's actions caused you.

You don't have to share anything that makes you uncomfortable or adds to your distress. However, isolation and loneliness can exacerbate anxiety, so staying connected is vital for your well-being.

Your loved ones can provide a listening ear when you need to talk about the thoughts that are causing you anxiety. They can also offer comfort and distraction when you're feeling overwhelmed. Even if you choose not to discuss the breakup, knowing you have someone who cares can significantly affect your thoughts.

Tips for Taking Care of Your Physical and Emotional Well-Being

Dealing with the aftermath of a breakup can be emotionally and physically challenging. It's normal to experience a range of feelings, from sadness and loneliness to anxiety and distress. During this period, taking care of your physical and emotional well-being is crucial. To enhance your overall wellness and manage the physical and emotional pain that often accompanies post-breakup anxiety, consider these strategies:

Physical Self-Care

Aim for 15 to 30 minutes of daily physical activity, preferably outdoors for sunlight and fresh air.

Stay Hydrated By Drinking Plenty Of Water

Avoid excessive alcohol consumption, as it can exacerbate anxiety.

Maintain regular eating habits, incorporating nutritious foods that can help reduce stress.

Establish a consistent sleep schedule, targeting 7 to 8 hours of sleep whenever possible.

Self-Care

- Spend 10 to 15 minutes daily in writing about your daily routine.

- Practice meditation to learn how to accept and cope with challenging emotions.

- Find Solace In Music.

- Dedicate time to relax and unwind each day.

- Allow yourself to grieve the loss without judgment.

- Discover a self-care routine that suits your needs.

Letting Go of the Need for Answers

It's common to have numerous questions after a breakup, primarily when your ex-partner didn't provide a satisfying explanation or if infidelity was involved. You might question your self-worth and wonder why the relationship didn't work. These thoughts can become repetitive and lead to uncertainty:

- What did I do wrong?

- Can I ever have a successful relationship?

- What if I run into them?

- Is it possible to get them back?

- How can I stop loving them?

- What should I tell people?

While finding answers might seem like the key to feeling good, it can trap you in a cycle of unpleasant emotions. Your ex might need clear explanations, and their responses might not provide the closure you seek. Reaching out to your ex can lead to prolonged uncertainty, an on-and-off relationship, and increased anxiety and distress. Moving forward without all the answers can be challenging, but focusing on your needs and values can help you let go of anxious thoughts. Eventually, you may reach a point where you no longer need to know why they ended the relationship.

Seeking Help from a Therapist
It's normal to feel anxious following a breakup. However, you should get treatment if it continues and begins to negatively impact your relationships, productivity at work or school, or general quality of life. Changes in physical health can also include headaches, stomach problems, altered appetite, and disturbed sleep. Breakups can cause a great deal of sorrow, so it's perfectly normal to look for more assistance. A therapist can help you identify the underlying causes of your emotional distress, offer coping mechanisms, and investigate variables that contribute to persistent emotional pain.

Remember that breakups can be incredibly challenging, and feeling anxious and lost during this time is okay. With time, even the most intense breakup grief can start to fade, creating a sense of calm and personal growth.

How to Stop Temptation Cope
Sometimes, people rush into a new relationship before recovering from their breakup. This type of relationship is called a rebound relationship. This relationship comes with many risks, but it does not mean it is meant to be a failed relationship. Let's look into the details of the rebound relationship.

Rebound Relationships

The simple definition of a rebound relationship means rushing into a new relationship before they are over their ex. After the breakup, we feel incomplete. To fill those gaps, we try to replace the old partner with a new one even though our feelings for the ex have not been resolved. When you are in a rebound relationship, you may think about your ex and wait for them to notice you are in a new relationship. However, it is worth noting that staying in that new one could be risky because of not coping with your feelings with your ex.

Are Rebound Relationships Risky?

According to popular opinions, rebound relationships fail because your new partner will soon realize you guys have nothing in common. You both will face instability in your relationship, no matter how much effort you both make.

Is it likely that relationships formed immediately after a breakup will not succeed? Clearly, 'rebound relationships' come with their own set of challenges.

The most significant risk is when someone enters a new relationship to escape the emotions tied to their previous one. They might rush into a new relationship to avoid the pain of a breakup and the following uncertainty. The problem is that these feelings tend to surface eventually, causing instability in the new relationship.

Another risk arises from how people choose their rebound partners. While it's commonly believed that they pick a new partner randomly, the reality is more complicated. They may choose someone who closely resembles their previous partner, physically or in terms of personality, or they might opt for someone entirely different.

Both scenarios have their problems. Choosing someone similar might mean trying to work out unresolved issues from the past, which can burden the new partner and lead to unpredictable resolutions. On the other hand, selecting someone very different can result in mismatched compatibility, especially once the initial 'honeymoon' phase ends.

However, when it comes to relationships, there are no strict rules. Rebound relationships have risks, but they aren't necessarily doomed to fail.

Many of us have seen cases where what some might call a classic 'rebound relationship' turns into a robust and lasting partnership. The truth is, it's tough to predict what will work. A seemingly perfect match on paper might not thrive in real life, and vice versa. Instead of setting rigid rules about what people should or shouldn't do, we should ask ourselves specific questions before deciding.

If you suspect you might be in a rebound relationship or are thinking about starting one, here are some things to consider:

How are you feeling? This can be a bit complicated, especially when dealing with a mix of emotions. Try to get a sense of where you stand about your previous relationship. Are you experiencing confusing emotions? Would your actions be driven by hurt or anger?

What do you want? Again, this can be tricky, but simply thinking about it can guide you towards an answer. Is there a particular direction you want to move in next? Conversely, are there paths you want to avoid?

What advice would you give to someone in your situation? Sometimes, it's helpful to step outside of yourself and look at things more objectively. If you were to talk to yourself about your current situation, what advice would you offer?

By reflecting on these questions, you can better understand your feelings and motivations in your current relationship and make more informed decisions about your romantic future.

Please Drop A Review

Dear Readers,

I hope you've been enjoying your journey through the pages of this book so far. As an author, my primary goal is to provide you with valuable insights, knowledge, or entertainment. Your feedback is incredibly important to me, as it helps me understand whether I've achieved that goal. Are you finding the content useful, thought-provoking, or simply enjoyable? Your opinions matter!

If you've been finding value in this book, I kindly request that you consider leaving a review of this book on Amazon. Your review can make a world of difference for other potential readers who are trying to decide if this book is the right fit for them. Your honest thoughts and opinions can guide them in making an informed choice. It's a small gesture that can have a big impact, and I genuinely appreciate your support. Thank you for being a part of this literary journey, and I look forward to hearing your thoughts.

4

Overcome Relief from Deep Emotional Pain

E veryone has different effects of a breakup; however, many people can benefit from therapy after their breakup. When you experience other emotions at once that are not in your control, therapy helps you cope with them, grieve the relationship, and adjust to a new journey in your life. Therapy is an additional support for you that enables you to heal the pain and move ahead in your life without looking back at what you have lost.

How Can Therapy Make a Difference?

Studies have shown that having a support system from friends and family significantly affects how well our relationships and overall well-being turn out. It can even affect our physical and mental health. So, when you're going through a breakup, the love and emotional backing from your loved ones can be a lifeline. But sometimes, that might not be enough. Your family might struggle to give you unbiased advice, or you might lack social connections. That's when professional help can become your best choice.

Therapy provides a safe space for you to navigate the emotional turmoil that follows a breakup. In therapy, a counselor assists you in recognizing any unhelpful ways you're dealing with the situation and helps you develop more effective coping strategies. These strategies could involve problem-solving, self-reflection, or relaxation techniques. The result? You learn to focus on your personal growth, manage the current situation, and carry these valuable skills into the future.

The role of a counselor is to help you grasp the negative emotions you're going through, change any irrational thoughts, set goals for the future, and create plans to achieve those goals. While friends and family might struggle to offer an unbiased perspective, mental health professionals are there to help you understand who you are, what you want in life, and how to boost your self-esteem following a breakup.

Breakups are a natural part of many romantic relationships and can take a toll on your emotions. Whether you were the one who initiated the breakup or the one it happened to, it's perfectly normal to feel a mix of emotions like sadness, anger, and confusion. But the good news is there are ways to help you deal with the aftermath of a breakup. And that's where therapy can become an invaluable tool in the healing process.

What Good Can Therapy Bring After a Breakup?
Therapy can be a beneficial resource for individuals going through a breakup. Here are some of the key ways it can benefit you:

Emotional Support
Therapy offers a safe and caring space to express and work through the emotions tied to the breakup. This helps you feel heard and understood, allowing you to deal with challenging feelings.

Gain Perspective
Therapy lets you see your situation from a fresh angle, helping you grasp the bigger picture. This can give you clarity and insight into your thoughts, emotions, and actions.

Develop Healthier Relationships
Therapy can assist you in recognizing patterns in your past relationships that may have contributed to the breakup. It

equips you with new skills for better communication and setting boundaries in future relationships.

Set Goals
With the help of a therapist, you can set goals for your life after the breakup. These might include boosting your self-esteem, exploring new interests, or strengthening relationships with family and friends. This way, you can focus on the future and find a sense of purpose post-breakup.

Coping Skills
Therapists can provide tools and techniques to handle the breakup's challenges. These may include managing stress, controlling your emotions, and enhancing your communication skills.

Address Underlying Issues
Finally, therapy can help you identify and tackle any underlying mental health concerns that might have played a role in the breakup, such as anxiety or depression.

So, as you can see, there are numerous benefits to seeking therapy after a breakup. By working with a trained therapist, you can navigate the challenges of a breakup and emerge from the experience with greater self-awareness, resilience, and hope for the future.

Therapies to Help You Heal After a Breakup

In today's world, professional counselors offer various therapies to assist clients in coping with the aftermath of a breakup. The most commonly used treatments worldwide include cognitive behavioral therapy (CBT), acceptance and commitment therapy (ACT), and psychotherapy. The choice of therapy depends on the specific challenges a client is facing.

For instance, if a client views the entire relationship as a traumatic experience and is struggling with post-traumatic stress following a breakup, therapists often opt for Eye Movement Desensitization and Reprocessing (EMDR). This therapy helps them process the trauma and work towards healing from the emotional distress caused by the troubling relationship.

On the other hand, if a breakup has left someone with low self-esteem, depression, or anxiety, Cognitive-Behavioral Therapy (CBT) might be the best choice. CBT is used to reframe unhelpful thought patterns and redefine future goals, fostering a healthier outlook.

If someone is finding it difficult to move on and cope with grief after a breakup, group counseling can be a great option. It provides an opportunity to hear others' stories, share their experiences, and realize they're not alone in their struggles.

Furthermore, there's the option of online therapy, where you can define your goals and select the most suitable treatment for your specific situation.

What is CBT?

CBT, or Cognitive Behavioral Therapy, is helpful when you're feeling down or anxious. It's like a guide to help you understand how your thoughts, actions, and feelings are connected. By figuring out these links, you can learn to think more positively and handle your emotions better, which can lead to positive changes in your life.

After a breakup, it's common to have negative thoughts like "I'm a failure" or "I'm unlovable." These thoughts can make you feel even worse and affect how you approach new relationships.

Here's where Cognitive Behavioral Therapy (CBT) makes a difference.

Cognitive Behavioral Therapy (CBT) is like a guide to help you deal with negative thoughts. It empowers you to change these unhelpful thought patterns into more positive ones. This means you can reshape your thoughts and feelings, moving towards becoming the person you want to be.

After a breakup, many people aim to find themselves again, create new routines, and imagine a brighter future. CBT provides valuable tools for fostering positive thoughts, adopting effective coping methods, and taking actions that align with your values. This helps you navigate the fear and sadness of a breakup, promoting personal growth and well-being.

Coping with a breakup through Cognitive Behavioral Therapy (CBT) involves various exercises to promote emotional well-being and personal growth. Here are some CBT exercises for dealing with the aftermath of a breakup:

Refocusing on Yourself

Cognitive refocusing is an effective CBT exercise. Whenever your thoughts drift back to your ex, consciously redirect your focus towards yourself. Reflect on your current activities and connections. Ask yourself questions like, "What am I doing right now?" and "Who am I connecting with apart from my ex?" This exercise allows you to shift your focus from what you've lost to the positive aspects of your life, including your relationships with friends and family.

Redefining Negative Thoughts

Another important CBT exercise is cognitive restructuring, which involves changing recurring negative or unhelpful thoughts into more balanced and neutral perspectives. For example, if you think, "I'll never be good enough for a relationship, and no one will ever love me again," reframe it as "I notice a fearful thought of being alone. I don't know what the future holds, but I'm feeling lonely right now, and reaching out to a friend for support might be a good idea."

Similarly, change thoughts like "I'm going to be single forever" to "I'll be single for a while." This statement acknowledges the current situation without damaging your self-esteem and emotions. Emilea Richardson suggests replacing thoughts like "I should have known better" with more constructive alternatives, such as, "I was doing the best I could with what I had at the time."

Breaking down the dynamics of a breakup and managing feelings of blame is essential to Cognitive Behavioral Therapy (CBT). Here are some strategies to help you navigate this process:

Breaking Down the Blame Game

Following a challenging breakup, it's common to either place all the blame on yourself or the other person. Emilea Richardson explains that CBT discourages this kind of black-and-white thinking, which tends to be unhelpful. Instead, Richardson suggests creating a "blame pie chart" to analyze and dissect the actions and responsibilities contributing to the relationship's breakdown. This approach encourages you to reconsider the breakup's events, break free from unhealthy thought patterns, and process what occurred, ultimately assisting you in coming to terms with the end of the relationship.

Exploring the Thoughts-Feelings-Behavior Triangle

The "thoughts-feelings-behavior triangle" is an exercise that can be done with a therapist or independently, as suggested by Richardson. In this exercise, you'll draw two triangles.

In the first triangle, write down the feelings, thoughts, and actions you are currently experiencing. Then, move on to the second triangle, where you'll note the feelings, opinions, or actions you wish you were experiencing instead.

For example, you may currently feel sad, lonely, discouraged, and afraid, but you desire to feel empowered, content, and hopeful. Ask yourself what is hindering you from experiencing these desired feelings. List the obstacles that might be holding you back, and you might discover that you have more control over your aspirational thoughts, feelings, and behaviors than you initially realized.

By breaking down blame and exploring your thoughts, feelings, and behaviors, you can better understand the breakup and work towards emotional healing and personal growth.

Managing overwhelming emotions and regaining control of your thoughts and actions after a breakup is integral to the healing process. Here are some strategies to help you in this regard:

Visualizing a Stop Sign

When you find yourself trapped in a cycle of negative thoughts, it can be beneficial to recognize the moment and regain control of your emotions. Imagine a vivid red stop sign as a symbol of that control. This mental image serves as a reminder that you have the power to steer your thoughts in a more positive direction. Victoria Smith suggests using this technique to guide your thoughts away from negativity gently. It's important to approach yourself with kindness as you shift your focus. Deep breathing while visualizing the stop sign can also provide a moment of peace, allowing your mind to regain its center and find calm.

Creating a Schedule of Activities

It's natural to want to spend time alone or in bed after a breakup, especially when dealing with stress and negative emotions. While it's okay in moderation, excessive isolation can hinder the experience of positive emotions. Brenda Arellano advises allowing yourself to feel good by scheduling activities you enjoy. This could involve spending time with friends and family, enjoying leisure activities, or simply walking in the park. Engaging in such activities can provide both enjoyment and distraction when needed. For example, changing your surroundings or participating in a different activity can help calm your mind and refocus your thoughts if you're overwhelmed by negative thoughts. These scheduled activities serve as a positive way to cope with the emotional challenges of a breakup.

Coping with Heartbreak and Rejection: How ACT Can Help

So, your relationship with your significant other has come to an end. You went through a rollercoaster of emotions, from numbness to the harsh reality of the breakup and the anger that followed. To make things worse, you found yourself scrolling through your ex's social media and stumbled upon a photo of them with someone new (who annoyingly happened to be quite attractive). Your mind starts playing tricks on you, making unfavorable comparisons between you and that new person. You even think, "I'll never find someone again, and I'll be lonely forever!" And to top it off, you believe these thoughts. You're sad and sorry for yourself but don't want to burden your friends with your ex-talk, so you withdraw from social interactions. Does this situation sound all too familiar?

Heartbreak is painful, and it becomes even more excruciating when it's accompanied by a sense of rejection, such as an unwanted breakup. Researchers have found that people experience similar brain activity when they look at a photo of their former partner as they do when they burn their arm, suggesting that heartbreak can be as emotionally painful as physical injury. Yet, heartbreak and rejection are shared experiences that most people go through unless they've wholly avoided relationships!

Acceptance and Commitment Therapy (ACT) can be remarkably helpful in coping with heartbreak and rejection. ACT focuses on accepting what's beyond your control, like others' actions, and taking practical steps to lead a meaningful life while managing the pain that comes with it. ACT achieves this in two primary ways:

Developing Psychological Skills

It helps you build psychological skills to manage your distressing thoughts and feelings more effectively, reducing their impact on you. Clarify your values as it assists you in identifying what is truly important and meaningful to you (your values) and then using that insight to guide your actions.

Let's explore how these ACT principles can be applied to cope with a breakup and rejection.

Practicing Mindfulness, Self-Compassion, and Defusion Skills

Breakups can be a whirlwind of painful emotions, including hurt, sadness, anger, frustration, and anxiety. Making space for these feelings and allowing yourself to experience them is crucial. Instead of fighting, denying, or suppressing your emotions, acknowledge them because when you try to push them down, they tend to return even stronger. Moreover, neglecting your own feelings or pretending they don't exist is self-invalidating. Imagine if you saw a child in distress or crying; you wouldn't ignore them, right? So why treat yourself any differently?

People often tend to avoid pain and downplay their suffering. The ability to acknowledge and respond to your discomfort with kindness is called "self-compassion," a central theme in ACT. However, self-compassion is something that only comes naturally to some people. Like any skill, it requires practice to improve.

Here are some practical steps to develop self-compassion:

Allow Yourself to Feel Your Feelings
Embrace your feelings until they naturally subside. Notice and describe your emotions, like saying, "I'm feeling sad/angry/hurt," and if you feel like crying, allow yourself to cry.

Normalize Crying
Remind yourself that crying is a normal reaction. It's perfectly okay to cry as much or as little as you need. Normalizing and validating your emotional responses is essential, so try it.

Treat Yourself as a Friend
Imagine how you would comfort and support a dear friend going through the same situation. Use the same words, tone of voice, gestures, and empathy to address yourself.

Next, let's talk about "Defusion Skills."
Defusion involves separating yourself from your thoughts, allowing them to come and go instead of getting entangled in them. During a breakup, you may experience negative thoughts and beliefs about not being worthy of love or not being good or important enough. This is because the human mind is naturally

inclined to think negatively. Our distant ancestors lived in a world full of constant dangers, where they could be attacked or killed by other animals at any moment. Consequently, our minds evolved to be vigilant for threats and to think negatively as a protective mechanism. "You'll be rejected" is the modern equivalent of "You'll get killed," in both cases, it's your mind's way of doing its primary job: protecting you and ensuring your survival.

Exploring Defusion Skills

Here are some techniques you can practice to defuse your negative thoughts:

I'm Having the Thought That...

State your negative thoughts, for example, "I'm not good enough."

Add the phrase "I'm having the thought that..." before it, like, "I'm having the thought that I'm not good enough."

Go one step further by saying, "I notice I'm having the thought that...," such as, "I notice I'm having the thought that I'm not good enough."

This simple exercise creates a separation from the thought. You're not eliminating the idea but acknowledging that it's just a thought, not a fact. This can weaken its hold on you.

Singing and Silly Voices

Formulate your negative thoughts or self-judgment in a brief sentence, e.g., "I'm a loser."

Internally, sing the thought to the tune of "Happy Birthday."

Then, hear the thought in the voice of a cartoon or movie character.

You can also say the thought out loud in a silly voice or exaggerated slow motion.

The objective here is to view the thought for what it truly is: a bunch of words that have entered your mind.

Letting Go Metaphors

Imagine your thoughts as if they are passing cars driving by your house, clouds drifting across the sky, waves gently washing onto the beach, trains arriving and departing from a station, or suitcases on a conveyor belt.

Please choose an image that resonates with you and practice letting your thoughts come and go without holding onto them.

The goal of defusion is not necessarily to feel better or eliminate unwanted thoughts. You can't stop your inner critic or silence your mind entirely, but you can strip these thoughts of their power over you.

Now, let's talk about EMDR Therapy.

EMDR Therapy

The goal of Eye Movement Desensitisation and Reprocessing (EMDR) therapy is to treat mental health conditions resulting from traumatic experiences. Although EMDR has been used to treat a wide range of other disorders, its most well-known use is in the treatment of post-traumatic stress disorder (PTSD).

EMDR therapy involves a specific technique where your eyes move in a particular way as you process traumatic memories to help you heal from trauma or distressing life experiences. While relatively new compared to other therapy methods, EMDR has demonstrated its effectiveness through numerous clinical trials dating back to 1989. EMDR is known for its ability to help individuals more rapidly than many other therapeutic approaches

Proven Effectiveness
Numerous studies have demonstrated the effectiveness of EMDR. It has a track record of helping individuals heal from traumatic experiences.

Faster Results
EMDR often produces quicker results compared to other therapy methods. Individuals undergoing EMDR therapy typically start experiencing improvements sooner than with alternative approaches.

Minimal Homework
EMDR therapy typically involves minimal homework. Instead of extensive journaling or additional assignments, you may only need to jot down any thoughts or ideas you want to discuss in your next session.

Reduced Stress
EMDR focuses on processing and moving beyond trauma without requiring you to describe or relive the traumatic events extensively. This can make the therapy experience less stressful compared to other methods that may involve revisiting distressing memories in great detail.

Understanding Adaptive Information Processing
EMDR therapy is rooted in the Adaptive Information Processing (AIP) model, a theory that explains how your brain stores memories. Developed by Francine Shapiro, the creator of EMDR, this model recognizes that the brain stores normal and traumatic memories differently.

In typical experiences, your brain smoothly stores memories and links them with related information. However, this networked storage process may not function correctly during traumatic events. It can lead to a disconnect between what you experience and how your brain encodes these experiences in memory.

Traumatic memories are often stored in a way that hinders healthy healing. These memories can be considered unhealed mental wounds, as the brain didn't receive the message that the danger had passed.

Furthermore, newer experiences may become linked to earlier traumatic experiences, reinforcing negative associations. This disruption affects the connections between your senses and memories, acting as an injury to the mind. Just as your body is sensitive to pain from physical damage, your mind can become hypersensitive to stimuli associated with trauma, leading to symptoms, emotions, and behaviors related to the traumatic experience.

This sensitivity isn't limited to conscious memories; it can also involve suppressed memories. Just as you've learned not to touch a hot stove because it burns, your mind tries to hide painful or distressing memories. However, this suppression is not perfect, and it can lead to the emergence of unfavorable symptoms, emotions, and behaviors.

Triggers and Overwhelming Memories
Senses signs such as sounds, sights, and smells related to any event that has occurred with you in the past and left a trauma can trigger stored traumatic memories. These triggers can result in overwhelming emotions such as anger, anxiety, fear, or panic.

For individuals with post-traumatic stress disorder (PTSD), improper storage and networking can result in flashbacks. During a flashback, the mind accesses traumatic memories in an uncontrolled, distorted, and overpowering way, making it feel as if the past is happening in the present.

Reprocessing and Healing

In EMDR therapy, you revisit memories of traumatic events in specific ways, often guided by eye movements and instructions. This process helps you reprocess the memories from an adverse event, allowing for a more adaptive and less distressing encoding of the experience.

Group Therapy for Breakups

Group therapy for breakups is a therapeutic approach where individuals who have experienced a breakup come together in a supportive and non-judgmental environment to share their experiences and emotions. Typically, a trained therapist leads the group, offering guidance and support. Group therapy can be particularly beneficial for those going through a breakup, as it provides a sense of community, reduces feelings of isolation, and reminds participants that they are not alone in their struggles. Additionally, it can be a more cost-effective option than individual therapy and offers a supportive network that extends beyond the therapy sessions.

There are various types of therapy for coping with breakups, and the most effective approach will depend on an individual's unique needs and preferences. Working with a trained therapist can offer valuable support and guidance throughout the healing process.

Icebreaker Activities

Group members learn about each other and create a comfortable and open atmosphere.

- Gratitude Activities: Participants may explore aspects of their lives they are thankful for, fostering a positive perspective.

- Sharing Activities: Group members engage in discussions

and ask each other questions to facilitate deeper understanding and empathy.

- Expressive Writing Activities: These encourage individuals to write about their experiences and emotions related to the breakup, providing a creative outlet for self-expression.

- Goal Visualization Activities: Group members may set goals and create plans for achieving them, promoting a sense of purpose and direction.

What Group Therapy Can Help With

It is a versatile approach that can be used to address various mental health conditions, including:

- Phobias

- Eating disorders

- Anxiety disorder

- Attention-deficit/hyperactivity disorder (ADHD)

- Depression

- Substance use disorder

- Panic disorder

- Post-traumatic stress disorder (PTSD)

Group therapy based on cognitive-behavioral therapy (CBT) principles has been found to be effective in helping people cope with challenges such as:

- Anger management

- Chronic pain

- Chronic illness

- Chronic stress

- Divorce

- Domestic violence

- Grief and loss

- Weight management

Group therapy offers a supportive and structured environment where individuals can learn from one another, share their experiences, and work toward their common goals. It can be a valuable resource for those facing various life challenges.

Choosing the Right Relationship Breakup Counselor

Selecting the right relationship breakup counselor is a pivotal step in healing. Here are some tips to help you make this decision effectively:

- Licensed Professional: Ensure that the counselor you choose is a licensed professional certified by a reputable organization.

- Experience: Seek a counselor with expertise in helping clients navigate breakups and other relationship challenges.

- Therapeutic Approach: Evaluate the counselor's therapeutic approach and verify that it aligns with your personal values and objectives.

- Reviews and Testimonials: Look for reviews and testimonials from previous clients to gain insight into their experiences working with the counselor.

- Trust Your Instincts: Trust your instincts when making this decision. It's essential to select a counselor with whom you feel comfortable and in whom you have confidence. Feel free to explore options until you find the right match for your unique needs.

Investing time in finding the ideal relationship breakup counselor can enhance your prospects of successfully navigating the healing process and emerging from the breakup with increased resilience and self-awareness.

What to Do When You're Tired of Everything

Acknowledging when you're tired of life and experiencing these signs is important. Once you recognize that you may be going through a difficult period, you can take steps to address these feelings and find a way to re-engage with life. Here are some tips to help you get out of the life you're tired of:

Seek Professional Help
If you feel extremely overwhelmed and these signs persist, consider seeking professional help. Mental health professionals provide you with guidance and support according to your situation.

Talk to Someone
Don't hesitate to confide in a trusted friend or family member about what you're going through. Sometimes, sharing your feelings and experiences with someone you trust can provide relief and valuable insights.

Set Small Goals

When you feel emotionally exhausted, set small, achievable goals for yourself. These can be as simple as taking a short walk, trying a new hobby, or spending quality time with a loved one. Small wins can build momentum and motivation.

Practice Self-Care

Take care of your physical and emotional well-being. This includes getting enough rest, eating nutritious foods, and engaging in activities that bring you joy and relaxation.

Mindfulness and Meditation

These practices can help you become more aware of your thoughts and emotions. They can also teach you how to stay present and focus on the current moment, reducing feelings of emotional numbness.

Explore Your Passions

Reconnect with the things you used to love or discover new interests and hobbies. Engaging in activities that bring you joy and fulfillment can reignite your passion for life.

Seek Support Groups

Consider joining a support group where you can connect with others who may be experiencing similar feelings. Sharing your experiences with people who understand can provide a sense of community.

Keep a Journal

Writing down your thoughts and emotions can be a therapeutic way to process your feelings and gain clarity about your experiences.

Remember that it's okay to ask for help and take the time you need to recover. Life can be challenging, but with the proper support and self-care, you can return to a more fulfilling and enjoyable life.

6 Tips to Help You Regain Your Liveliness

If you're feeling tired of life and want to regain your liveliness, these tips can help you on your journey to a more fulfilling and vibrant life. Remember that it's okay to seek professional help if you find implementing these changes on your own challenging. Here are the steps to follow:

Picture Your Ideal Life
Imagine the life you would love to lead. Consider factors like your environment, the people around you, and your mental and emotional well-being. Take your time to visualize this ideal life.

Look Back on Your Most Enjoyable Times
Reflect on the moments in your past when you felt most alive and fulfilled. Think about the activities, people, and circumstances that contributed to your happiness during those times.

Identify What's Missing
From your ideal life and enjoyable past experiences, determine what's currently missing from your life. These are the elements you want to reintroduce or enhance.

Focus on What's Within Your Control
Highlight the aspects you believe are within your control, such as changing your career, relationships, or living environment. Develop a plan to work on these areas one step at a time.

Address What Seems Out of Your Control
For the aspects that seem beyond your control, look for second-best alternatives or ways to adapt and find contentment despite limitations. Sometimes, small adjustments can lead to meaningful improvements.

Set Meaningful Goals
The purpose of life should be to live, not survive. Establish your goals that align with the vision of your ideal life. Ensure your

goals are SMART, specific, measurable, achievable, relevant, and time-bound. When you have a plan in your life, you can have a purpose and something to strive that is worth spending for.

Implementing these steps can help you regain your zest for life and work towards a more fulfilling future. Additionally, focus on self-care, reaching out to supportive friends and family, and allowing yourself to grieve and heal from past experiences. By following these strategies and making gradual changes, you can rediscover the liveliness and purpose in your life.

5

Venture Into Gaining Self-Confidence

"When we love, we always strive to become better than we are. When we strive to become better than we are, everything around us becomes better, too."

Paulo Coelho

P aula Coelho made a very insightful statement that is especially relevant for people trying to rediscover who they are. Moving past a relationship is only one aspect of love; another is loving oneself.

After heartbreaks, we can occasionally get lost and stop becoming the people we once were. However, during these exposed moments, we are given a unique opportunity to learn that we can fall in love again, this time with ourselves, not with anyone else.

Sometimes, after heartaches, we lose our way and become strangers to the ones we used to be. Yet, in these moments of openness, we are presented with a unique opportunity: an opportunity to see that we can fall in love again, this time not for someone else, but for yourself."

When we fight to be above who we are, we change the world, and we, too, change. Self-love makes it easy to move past a breakup and improve all you see and do. Therefore, let's begin this journey with an open mind and heart.

This chapter will discuss love, with self-love being the ultimate expression or fulfillment of that emotion. It will teach you how to reignite the spark of old dreams, redouble your passion for dancing, and turn your compassion toward yourself into a vehicle of change. Love yourself, and you will reach deeply into your actual layers and find that strength and resilience and pleasure within you and about you, yourself.

Reflecting into Self-Rediscovery

The beginning of your new life, my journey with you to discover yourself. I understand you are also facing some challenges. Though heartbreak can make you feel like you don't know what to do, there is always a silver lining. It is a journey of self-discovery to get to know your true self and understand what is needed of you in life.

Let me start by saying that you are not alone. Many people, including myself, have gone through what you're going through now. It's all a part of the process: the pain, the confusion. But it is also the beginning of the most beautiful thing in the world: a journey back to yourself.

We can begin by discussing what you enjoy most in life. Reflect on the things you used to enjoy before. For example, you might have loved painting, writing, or playing an instrument like music. Now is the period to rekindle those long-lost passions. They are not mere entertainment but expressions of your inner essence that will fill you with profound happiness.

Discovering your identity is just another way of saying rediscovering yourself. They impact every decision that you take or action that you make. Knowing them is essential because it helps to match your life to what speaks to you, giving your life more authenticity and meaning.

This is not about changing into a new person. That is all that it has to do with. You will return home in that regard to the man you have had within yourself beneath these roles and expectations. It's all about holding on and walking on purpose.

However, after a breakup or divorce, we need to take some time and examine ourselves, not just ourselves as partners. This self-introspection is not meant to assign blame but to develop and learn. Here are some profound questions to help you on this journey:

1. Knowing your role in the relationship dynamics is crucial: Take a breath, zoom out, and look more comprehensively at your past relationship. Remember, how did your group bring in the hardships? Could your behavior or reactions have provoked some misunderstanding? Creating a conflict? Self-awareness, the willingness to accept one's part in relationship dynamics and its effects on oneself, is not self-blame.

2. Recognizing Patterns in Your Relationships: Review your past relationships. Do you detect any pattern in the choices you make? Do you make the same type of people the victims or repeat the same mistakes in each of your novels and short stories? This will help to identify these patterns so that the cycle can be broken and better decisions can be made in the future.

3. Assessing Your Coping Mechanisms: Consider how you deal with stress, conflicts, and fears. Do you amplify situations by intensifying them through your reactions or take them to a new level of resolution and evolution? Thinking of it can also enable you to develop more positive approaches to your problems in relationships and at large.

4. Accepting Others as They Are: Consider your expectations of others. Do you often find yourself needing to "fix" the people in your life, or is it OK to live with their imperfections? Acceptance and understanding, not the hope of what someone could be or should be, is what relationships are fed upon.

5. Gaining Mastery over Your Emotions: Determine the kind of negative emotions you are experiencing. How transient are they, or do they control your mood and your view? It is the first step in learning to control your emotions rather than letting them control you. It can be a basis for profound personal change.

6. Reflecting on Self-Improvement: It is also a great time to think about certain aspects of your life that you'd like to enhance or modify after going through a separation. This is about more than being better for them in the future; it is about being your best self for you.

7. Evaluating Your Growth and Happiness: Consider what gives your life and brings joy. How can you add more of these things to your life? After-breakup should lead to personal discovery and define one's direction toward personal satisfaction.

Finding Your Passions
After a breakup, people feel lost and detached from themselves. The other option is to take the highway out of the abyss by renewing past experiences, old passions, or hobbies one would like to revisit. A lot of profits resulting from pursuits can be helpful in additional steps to improve their state.

Physical Benefits
Engaging in physical hobbies like hiking, gardening, and dancing offers numerous health benefits beyond just the physical aspect. These activities promote cardiovascular fitness, muscle strength,

flexibility, and balance, improving overall physical health. Hiking, for instance, provides a great cardiovascular workout and allows you to connect with nature, reducing stress and enhancing mental well-being. Gardening not only strengthens muscles and burns calories but also fosters a sense of accomplishment and relaxation as you nurture and care for plants. On the other hand, dancing combines physical exercise with the joy of self-expression, releasing endorphins and reducing anxiety.

Moreover, these physical hobbies can significantly impact your emotional and psychological well-being. Engaging in these activities can be therapeutic when going through a tough time, such as a breakup. Physical exercise, in particular, triggers the release of endorphins, which are natural mood lifters. This can help alleviate sadness, boost self-esteem, and enhance your emotional state. Additionally, the focus required for hobbies like gardening and dancing can serve as a healthy distraction, allowing you to temporarily escape from distressing thoughts and find solace in the present moment. Ultimately, the combination of physical and mental benefits that these hobbies provide can aid in the healing process and help you recover faster from emotional setbacks like a breakup.

Mental Benefits
Hobbies are crucial in promoting positive mental well-being and reducing stress in our lives. Engaging in activities we are passionate about and enjoy can bring immense joy and satisfaction. When we pursue hobbies, we immerse ourselves in activities that provide a sense of purpose and fulfillment, contributing to increased happiness and reduced stress levels.

Hobbies also serve as an excellent means of relaxation and escape from the demands and pressures of daily life. They create a healthy diversion, allowing us to detach from stressors and worries temporarily. Whether it's painting, playing a musical instrument, cooking, or any other hobby, concentrating on a creative or enjoyable task can induce a state of flow where time seems to slip away, and our minds are fully absorbed in the present moment. This mindfulness-like experience can be incredibly calming and therapeutic, helping to alleviate stress and anxiety.

Emotional Benefits

Engaging in activities that you genuinely enjoy can bring about a wide array of emotional benefits. When you do things that make you happy and fulfill you, you often experience a heightened sense of positivity and contentment. This positive emotional state can lead to increased feelings of joy, satisfaction, and overall well-being.

Additionally, pursuing activities you love can serve as a powerful stress-relief mechanism. Engaging in enjoyable hobbies or pastimes can help reduce anxiety and tension, as they provide a healthy outlet for stress and distract you from worries and negative thoughts. Whether reading a book, playing a sport, creating art, or spending time with loved ones, these activities can trigger the release of feel-good neurotransmitters like dopamine and serotonin, which can help alleviate stress and promote emotional balance.

Doing things you enjoy often fosters a sense of purpose and meaning. It can boost your self-esteem and self-worth as you experience a sense of accomplishment and mastery within your chosen activities. This, in turn, can enhance your emotional resilience and provide you with a valuable source of motivation and positivity, ultimately contributing to a more fulfilling and emotionally satisfying life. Social and Interpersonal

Hobbies are a source of personal enjoyment and a fantastic avenue for expanding your social network and connecting with like-minded individuals. When you engage in hobbies that interest you, you are more likely to encounter people who share your passion and enthusiasm for those activities. This common ground forms a strong foundation for building new friendships and relationships. Whether you're into gardening, painting, hiking, or playing a musical instrument, participating in hobby-related groups, clubs, or online communities allows you to meet people who share your interests, opening up opportunities for meaningful connections.

Creativity
Hobbies encourage creativity. They also let people be creative and think out of the box. These are done in writing or crafts. Another activity that one can take part in is cooking.

Schedule Free Time
Dedicate some specific hours for your free time. Consider this your most important appointment and treat it in such a manner.

How to Choose a Hobby

Hobbies vs. Interests
Hobbies are not just something you like but also something you do. However, consider the differences it could make for you before selecting an interest.

Finding Inspiration
What is that one thing you've always wanted to do? Recall your early desires and wonder, for instance, what gives you pleasure in playtime. The saying "daily inspiration" can work every day. Therefore, look for the ones you already like, such as cooking, decorations, and reading. This can be motivated by attending meetings, different clubs, or through class. Hobbies are personal. They should be the source of happiness and fulfillment. Lastly, do not fear experimenting with something; you have to derive pleasure as you explore yourself.

Reflecting on 10 Questions for Healthy Distraction.

However, engaging in some healthy distractions or hobbies is vital during this self-discovery journey. More than just a break, they are part of personal development. I have designed a reflective worksheet to help you select a hobby that aligns with your authentic self. The 10-item questionnaire will help you trace your interests and inclinations toward a genuine pursuit.

1. Joy in Competition: Do challenges excite you? Think of whether competition increases the pleasure of your profession.

2. Solo or Social: Do you feel at peace while doing the activities, or do you find energy while interacting socially? Such preference will point you towards a social hobby that will satisfy your social needs.

3. Skill Enhancement: Do you have any skills or talents you want to learn or improve? Think of the hobbies that can help develop this skill.

4. Physical Engagement: Reflect on your lifestyle. Would a little exercise work? Therefore, you should pursue sports and other fitness-based activities as a hobby.

5. Childhood Revisited: Remember when you were young? Have you participated in activities you loved before but now gave them up? Finding back to these can be enjoyable and exciting.

6. Creative Outlets: Waiting for your creative fire! Creative hobbies such as painting, writing, or crafting are very satisfying.

7. Nature's Call: Are you attracted to the great outdoors?

Your hobby could include activities such as hiking, gardening, and bird-watching.

8. Learning and Knowledge: Do you long to quench your thirst for knowledge? For your intellectual curiosity, you can go for hobbies such as reading, workshops, or museums.

9. Relaxation and Calm: Are you one of those who search for soothing leisure activities that give a pleasant feeling? Try yoga, meditation, knitting, or anything to find peace.

10. Giving Back: Do you feel warm when contributing to the community? You may also think of some hobbies that involve volunteering or community services.

11. This worksheet, take it slow. Pause, think through each question, and describe your emotions and thoughts. This is not about right or wrong answers but for insights leading you to a hobby that brings happiness and growth, and you will be honest about yourself. This is an exciting discovery process, so enjoy it as there is another stage in your fascinating journey towards self-discovery.

To conclude this chapter in Reflecting into Self-Rediscovery, let us pause and review ourselves. It is a transformational journey where we are connecting to old hobbies and remembering long-lost dreams. Firstly, we have come a long way in discovering our actual being.

Through interactive exercises and reflective worksheets, we have dug deep into your likes, childhood fantasies, and potential new skills that have never been imagined. Every step was aimed at moving you toward your inner self to grow personally and realize who you are.

It is not over as we turn the page. It's just beginning. Then follows the next chapter, "Rebuilding Self-Belief," as your step towards healing and empowerment.

After a breakup, one often feels less worthy and incomplete. The following chapter is intended to deal directly with these particular challenges. These exercises will also be a practical and life-changing effect on your confidence. Reframing limiting beliefs will help you view yourself in more empowering ways.

Think of your improved version of yourself who stands straight and proud, with confidence and self-confidence. It is not a far cry because you are more than capable of achieving it. The next chapter is your map for reclaiming the inner self-esteem and self-confidence lying dormant in you.

Prepare yourself for this new portion of your journey. On each page, you will discover that strength you never knew you had and the wisdom ready to come up. As you proceed with this journey of self-improvement and recovery, there are many things to look forward to.

6
Empowering Self Belief

N avigating through the aftermath of a breakup can indeed be an emotional rollercoaster, and it's crucial to acknowledge and accept the wide range of emotions you may experience during this challenging period. It's entirely normal to feel a mix of sadness, anger, confusion, and even moments of relief. These emotions can come and go like waves, making the journey through a breakup uniquely challenging and sometimes exhausting. Giving yourself permission to grieve and process these emotions without judgment is essential.

One critical aspect of post-breakup recovery is recognizing signs of low self-esteem that may surface as a result of the emotional upheaval. A breakup can often lead to feelings of rejection and inadequacy, which can profoundly impact one's self-worth. Some common signs of low self-esteem in the aftermath of a breakup include a negative self-image, constant self-criticism, a tendency to blame oneself for the relationship's failure, and seeking external validation to feel valued. These signs can create a cycle of negative self-talk and further erode your self-esteem.

Acknowledging these signs is a crucial step towards healing and rebuilding your self-esteem. Self-awareness allows you to identify the areas where you may be struggling and address them proactively. It's important to remind yourself that a breakup does not define your worth and it's an opportunity for personal growth and self-discovery.

Ultimately, healing from a breakup is a journey, and recognizing signs of low self-esteem is the first step toward finding strength and resilience within yourself. Let's take a closer look at some of these signs:

Avoiding Challenges and Opportunities

After a breakup, feeling apprehensive about taking on new challenges is common. However, if you consistently avoid opportunities that come your way, it might be a sign that your self-esteem needs a boost. Remember, challenges can be stepping stones to personal growth.

Avoiding Responsibilities
A sense of being overwhelmed might lead to avoiding responsibilities. If you notice yourself steering clear of tasks you once handled easily, it could indicate low self-esteem. Tackling responsibilities, even in small steps, can be a powerful way to regain a sense of control.

Being Overly Dependent on Others
Dependency on others for emotional support is natural, but it might indicate a dip in self-esteem when it becomes excessive. Building a support network is crucial, but focusing on your emotional well-being is equally important.

Relying on Others to Make Decisions
If you consistently rely on others to make decisions for you, it may suggest a lack of confidence in your judgment. Start small by making minor decisions independently to rebuild trust in yourself gradually.

Putting Yourself Down
Negative self-talk can be a powerful influencer of self-esteem. If you catch yourself constantly putting yourself down or engaging

in self-criticism, it's time to change that narrative. Practice self-compassion and focus on your strengths.

Isolating Yourself
Feeling the need to withdraw from social interactions is common after a breakup, but prolonged isolation can contribute to low self-esteem. Gradually reintroduce social activities into your life to reconnect with others and build a sense of belonging.

Becoming Highly Emotional, Possibly Depressed
Experiencing heightened emotions post-breakup is normal, but if you find yourself sinking into prolonged periods of sadness or depression, it's crucial to seek support. Professional help or talking to friends and family can make a significant difference.

Remember, recognizing these signs is the first step toward positive change. Be patient with yourself, and consider seeking support from friends, family, or professionals to navigate this challenging time.

How Long Does It Take to Recover Self-Esteem After a Breakup?

Navigating the path to self-esteem recovery after a breakup is a unique journey for each individual. According to studies cited in the article from spring.org.uk, the timeline for rebuilding self-esteem can vary. Factors such as the length and intensity of the relationship, the nature of the breakup, and individual coping mechanisms all contribute to the duration of the recovery process.

Research suggests that it may take weeks to months for some individuals to see improvements in self-esteem post-breakup. The key lies in understanding that healing is a gradual process with no one-size-fits-all timeline. Now, let's uncover some effective strategies supported by these studies to help boost your self-esteem along the way.

Tips on Raising Self-Esteem After a Breakup

Self-Reflection and Acceptance

Self-reflection and acceptance are pivotal components of the healing process after a breakup. It's essential to create space for introspection and allow yourself to delve into your emotions without criticism or self-blame. This process of self-reflection can help you gain clarity about the relationship, your needs and desires, and the lessons you can take away from the experience. By confronting your feelings and acknowledging the pain and sadness that a breakup can bring, you're permitting yourself to grieve, and this emotional release is an integral part of the healing journey.

Acceptance is a powerful force in rebuilding self-esteem. It involves acknowledging the reality of the situation and recognizing that breakups are a natural part of life. Instead of dwelling on what could have been or assigning blame, accepting the end of the relationship allows you to begin moving forward. Remembering that a breakup does not define your worth or your ability to love and be loved in the future is essential. Acceptance opens the door to self-compassion, a crucial element in rebuilding self-esteem. As you treat yourself with kindness and understanding, you nurture a healthier self-image and rebuild the confidence the breakup may have shaken.

Set Realistic Goals

Setting realistic and attainable goals is crucial for rebuilding self-esteem, especially after a breakup. Begin by breaking down your larger objectives into smaller, manageable steps. These small goals can span various aspects of your life, from personal to professional, and can serve as building blocks for your self-esteem recovery journey.

Accomplishing even the most modest tasks can provide a significant sense of achievement and boost your confidence.

These small victories prove that you can take control of your life and make progress, fostering a positive self-image. For instance, you might set a goal to engage in a new hobby, complete a work project, or maintain a daily routine that includes exercise and self-care. As you achieve these goals, you'll regain faith in your abilities and recognize your intrinsic worth, gradually counteracting the negative impact of the breakup on your self-esteem.

Setting realistic goals helps you regain a sense of purpose and direction. It can provide structure and motivation during a period when you may feel adrift or uncertain about your future. By focusing on these achievable objectives, you're actively investing in your own well-being and personal growth, which can be incredibly empowering and contribute to a more positive outlook on life after a breakup.

Positive Affirmations
Positive affirmations are a powerful tool for countering negative self-talk and boosting self-esteem, especially in the aftermath of a breakup. These are positive statements or phrases that you can repeat to yourself regularly, helping to reshape your inner dialogue and focus on your strengths and accomplishments. When dealing with low self-esteem after a breakup, it's common for negative thoughts to dominate your mind, such as feeling unworthy or unlovable. Positive affirmations can act as a counterbalance, reminding you of your inherent worth and capabilities.

By consciously challenging negative self-talk with positive affirmations, you are actively working to shift your perspective. Instead of fixating on your perceived flaws or shortcomings, you redirect your attention to your qualities and achievements. For example, if you find yourself thinking, "I'm not good enough," you can counteract this thought with an affirmation like, "I am deserving of love and respect." Over time, these affirmations can help rewire your brain, gradually replacing self-doubt with self-confidence.

Incorporating positive affirmations into your daily routine can be a simple yet effective practice. You can write them down in a journal, repeat them in front of a mirror, or use them as daily mantras. The key is consistency and patience, as these affirmations may take time to impact your self-esteem significantly. Nevertheless, they can be a valuable tool in your journey towards healing and rebuilding your self-worth after a breakup. Build a Support System

Connect with friends, family, or support groups. Surrounding yourself with positive influences can provide encouragement and perspective during challenging times.

Engage in Activities You Enjoy
Rediscover hobbies and activities that bring you joy. Investing time in things you love can enhance your fulfillment and happiness.

Seek Professional Support
Consider talking to a therapist or counselor. Professional guidance can offer valuable insights and coping strategies tailored to your situation.

Practice Self-Care
Prioritize self-care to nurture your physical and emotional well-being. Adequate sleep, a balanced diet, and regular exercise contribute to overall wellness.

Remember, the journey toward rebuilding self-esteem is gradual, and progress may not always be linear. Be patient with yourself, celebrate small victories, and embrace the support available to you. With time and self-care, you'll find yourself on a path to renewed self-esteem and a brighter future.

Strategies to Boost Self-Esteem After a Breakup

Appreciate Yourself - Gift of Self-Care

In the journey to rebuilding self-esteem, it's crucial to appreciate yourself. Take intentional breaks to relax and unwind, treating yourself to a 'gift' of self-care. Whether it's a quiet moment with a good book or a rejuvenating walk, these small gestures can go a long way in nurturing your well-being.

Accepting Limitations with Compassion

Acknowledge that everyone has limitations, and that's perfectly okay. Embrace your imperfections with compassion rather than judgment. Understand that these limitations are a part of what makes you uniquely human, and they don't diminish your worth.

Silencing Self-Criticism

One of the most impactful ways to raise self-esteem is to end self-criticism. Challenge the inner voice that speaks negatively about yourself. Replace harsh words with self-compassion, acknowledging that everyone makes mistakes and experiences setbacks.

Recognizing Achievements and Strengths

Reflect on your accomplishments and strengths. Recognize the hurdles you've overcome and the skills you possess. Remind yourself of instances where you have succeeded, reinforcing the belief in your capabilities.

Pampering Yourself

Self-care is not a luxury; it's a necessity. Pamper yourself with activities that bring joy and relaxation. Whether it's a soothing bath, a favorite meal, or a creative pursuit, these moments contribute to a positive sense of self.

Focusing on Positive Feelings

Shift your focus to positive feelings by recalling times when you were genuinely happy, relaxed, and at peace. Visualization of these moments can create a reservoir of positivity, serving as a source of strength during challenging times.

Accepting Compliments Gracefully

Accepting compliments gracefully is essential to bolster your self-esteem, especially during the healing process after a breakup. It involves acknowledging the kind words or recognition from others and genuinely internalizing and believing in the positive feedback you receive. When someone compliments your strengths or accomplishments, it's a moment to embrace and celebrate your worth. Instead of brushing it off or downplaying your achievements, take a moment to thank the person genuinely.

By accepting compliments gracefully, you are actively reinforcing a more positive self-image. It's a way of counteracting the negative self-talk that often accompanies low self-esteem, particularly in the wake of a breakup. When you allow yourself to believe the positive feedback from others, you begin to challenge the self-doubt and self-criticism that might have emerged from the relationship's end. Over time, this practice can contribute to a more resilient and confident self-concept, helping you regain your sense of worth and self-assuredness. So, the next time someone pays you a compliment, receive it with an open heart and a grateful spirit, for it is a step toward rebuilding your self-esteem and embracing a more positive self-image.

Reminding Yourself of Your Good Qualities

Regularly remind yourself of your good qualities and past successes. This practice helps counteract self-doubt and builds a foundation of confidence rooted in self-awareness.

Embracing the Grey Areas

Avoid thinking in black-and-white terms. Life is nuanced, and so are your experiences. Embrace the grey areas, allowing for complexity and growth in your journey of self-discovery.

Setting Realistic Goals

Set achievable and realistic goals. Break down larger objectives into manageable steps, celebrating each milestone. This gradual progress contributes to a sense of accomplishment.

Starting an Exercise Regimen
Physical activity has profound effects on mental well-being. Initiate an exercise routine that suits your preferences, whether a brisk walk, yoga, or dancing. The endorphin release can significantly uplift your mood.

Practicing Kindness to Yourself
Be kind to yourself, treating your inner dialogue with the same kindness you extend to others. Self-compassion is a powerful tool in cultivating a positive self-image.

Recognizing Positives
Train your mind to recognize positives. Even in challenging situations, there are often silver linings. Cultivate an attitude of gratitude, focusing on what you can learn and gain from each experience.

Building a Support Network
Surround yourself with a supportive network of friends, family, or a support group. Sharing your thoughts and feelings with others can provide valuable perspectives and encouragement.

Try Talk Therapy
Consider talking therapy as a proactive step toward healing. Professional guidance can offer insights and coping strategies tailored to your needs, fostering emotional resilience.

Setting Personal Challenges
Challenge yourself by setting personal goals that align with your interests and passions. No matter how small, each accomplishment contributes to a sense of purpose and achievement.

Harnessing the Power of Therapy to Cultivate Self-Esteem

In self-esteem cultivation, therapy emerges as a potent and transformative tool. As explored on positivepsychology.com, therapy provides a nuanced and structured approach to building self-esteem. Let's delve into how therapy can be a cornerstone in your journey towards enhanced confidence and self-worth.

Creating a Supportive Alliance
Therapy offers a safe and non-judgmental space where individuals can forge a supportive alliance with a trained professional. This therapeutic relationship becomes a crucial pillar, providing validation, empathy, and a foundation for self-exploration.

Unveiling Underlying Issues
Skilled therapists guide individuals through uncovering and understanding the root causes of low self-esteem. By delving into past experiences and exploring thought patterns, therapy unveils the layers that contribute to self-esteem challenges.

Challenging Negative Beliefs
A pivotal aspect of therapy involves identifying and challenging negative beliefs about oneself. Therapists employ evidence-based techniques to reframe negative thought patterns, fostering a more positive and realistic self-perception.

Developing Coping Strategies
Therapy equips individuals with practical coping strategies to navigate challenges and setbacks. By building a toolkit of effective coping mechanisms, individuals gain the resilience to confront difficulties and maintain a healthier self-esteem.

Setting Personalized Goals
Goals are tailored to the individual's unique needs and aspirations in the therapeutic setting. Therapists collaborate with clients to set realistic and achievable objectives, creating a roadmap for personal growth and self-esteem enhancement.

Enhancing Self-Awareness
Therapy facilitates deep self-reflection, fostering heightened self-awareness. Through guided exploration, individuals gain insight into their emotions, behaviors, and thought processes, laying the groundwork for positive change.

Building Assertiveness Skills
For many, low self-esteem is intertwined with difficulties expressing needs and boundaries. Therapy provides a platform to develop assertiveness skills, empowering individuals to communicate effectively and advocate for themselves.

Encouraging Positive Visualization
Therapists often integrate techniques such as positive visualization, encouraging individuals to envision their future selves with higher self-esteem. This forward-looking approach helps instill hope and motivation for positive change.

Promoting Self-Compassion
Central to self-esteem development is the cultivation of self-compassion. Therapy encourages individuals to treat themselves with kindness and understanding, fostering a nurturing inner dialogue that counteracts self-criticism.

Incorporating Mindfulness Practices
Mindfulness, a cornerstone of many therapeutic approaches, is integrated to enhance self-awareness and present-moment acceptance. Mindfulness practices empower individuals to observe thoughts and feelings without judgment, promoting a healthier relationship with oneself.

Encouraging Interpersonal Exploration
Therapy extends beyond individual introspection, often delving into interpersonal dynamics. Exploring relationships and communication patterns allows individuals to develop healthier connections, positively impacting their sense of self.

Providing a Framework for Growth

Ultimately, therapy serves as a dynamic framework for personal growth. By addressing self-esteem within the therapeutic context, individuals are guided toward a more profound understanding of themselves, fostering lasting confidence and resilience.

As you consider therapy a tool for enhancing self-esteem, it's essential to recognize the transformative potential within this collaborative and supportive process. The insights gained, and skills developed in therapy can catalyze positive change, laying the groundwork for a more confident and self-assured version of yourself.

Elevating Self-Esteem: 8 Skills and Techniques to Embrace

Embarking on a journey to boost self-esteem involves cultivating diverse skills and techniques. Let's explore eight empowering interventions that can become valuable additions to your arsenal.

Practice Mindfulness

Mindfulness, the art of being present in the moment without judgment, is a potent tool for self-esteem. As Jon Kabat-Zinn, a pioneer in mindfulness research, wisely puts it, "You can't stop the waves, but you can learn to surf." Practicing mindfulness allows you to navigate the waves of self-doubt with grace, fostering a deeper connection with the present and a more compassionate relationship with yourself.

Change Your Story

Challenge and reshape the narrative you tell yourself. As renowned psychologist Albert Ellis suggests, "You largely constructed your depression. It wasn't given to you. Therefore, you can deconstruct it." Empower yourself by reframing negative self-talk into positive affirmations, creating a narrative emphasizing resilience and growth.

Don't Compare Yourself to Others

In the words of Theodore Roosevelt, "Comparison is the thief of joy." Recognize that your journey is uniquely yours. Embrace your individuality, focusing on personal growth rather than measuring yourself against others. This shift in perspective fosters a more authentic sense of self-worth.

Channel That Inner Rock Star

Tap into your strengths and celebrate your achievements, no matter how small. In the words of Maya Angelou, "You may not control all the events that happen to you, but you can decide not to be reduced by them." Acknowledge your accomplishments, channel your inner rock star, and revel in the music of your achievements.

Move Your Body More

Physical activity is a powerful catalyst for positive mental health. As the ancient proverb says, "A healthy body breeds a healthy mind." Engage in activities that bring you joy, whether dancing, hiking, or yoga. Moving your body enhances physical well-being and contributes to a positive self-image.

Volunteer

Contributing to the well-being of others can be a profound self-esteem booster. Winston Churchill once remarked, "We make a living by what we get, but we make a life by what we give." Volunteer work provides a sense of purpose and accomplishment, fostering a positive outlook on your capabilities.

Practice Forgiveness

Forgiveness is a gift you give to yourself. In the words of Maya Angelou, "It's one of the greatest gifts you can give yourself, to forgive. Forgive everybody." Letting go of resentment and self-blame liberates your mind, paving the way for self-compassion and healthier self-esteem.

Realize That You Are Not Your Circumstances

Eleanor Roosevelt's insight, "You gain strength, courage, and confidence by every experience in which you stop to look fear in the face," emphasizes the transformative power of challenges. Recognize that your circumstances do not define you. You have the strength to face adversity and emerge stronger.

Integrating these skills and techniques into your life builds a robust foundation for enhanced self-esteem. Remember, self-esteem is a journey, not a destination. Embrace these interventions with patience and commitment, and watch as they contribute to the flourishing of your confidence and self-worth.

Building Unshakeable Self-Belief: A Road to Recovery After a Breakup

Navigating the aftermath of a breakup involves healing emotional wounds and rebuilding the pillars of self-worth. Drawing insights from lifehack.org and forbes.com, let's embark on a journey of confidence-building exercises tailored to healing and repairing self-worth.

Create a Strong Personal Belief Statement

Craft a personal belief statement that reflects your values, strengths, and aspirations. Use positive language to affirm your worth and potential. Regularly revisit and recite this statement as a source of inspiration and motivation.

Practice, Practice, Practice

Identify specific skills or activities related to your personal or professional growth. Devote consistent time and effort to practice these, acknowledging that improvement comes with dedicated repetition. Celebrate the progress made, reinforcing your competence.

Surround Yourself With Confident and Competent People
Cultivate a supportive social circle. Engage with individuals who exude confidence and competence. Observe and learn from their behaviors, allowing their positivity to influence and uplift your self-belief.

Keep Track of Your Wins
Maintain a Wins Journal where you document your achievements, no matter how small. Reflecting on past successes reinforces a positive self-narrative and is a tangible reminder of your capabilities.

Trust in the Greater Universality of Life
Embrace the understanding that setbacks and challenges are universal experiences. Recognize that overcoming difficulties is a shared human journey, fostering a sense of connection and resilience in the face of adversity.

Conquer Your Inner Critic
Identify and challenge negative self-talk. Whenever your inner critic surfaces, counteract it with positive affirmations and evidence of your strengths. Develop a habit of self-encouragement to drown out self-doubt.

Reflect on Accomplishments
Set aside time for regular self-reflection. Acknowledge and appreciate your accomplishments, recalling the efforts invested and the skills demonstrated. This reflective practice reinforces a positive self-image.

Maintain Good Posture
Pay attention to your body language. Stand tall, maintain eye contact, and project confidence through your posture. The physical act of adopting a strong posture can influence your mental perception of self-assurance.

Develop an Equality Mentality
Recognize the inherent worth and equality of all individuals. Shift away from comparisons that breed insecurity and embrace a mindset that values everyone's unique strengths and contributions.

Try Things That Make You Uncomfortable
Challenge yourself by deliberately engaging in activities that push your boundaries. Lifehack suggests that embracing discomfort fosters adaptability and resilience. Stepping into the unknown builds confidence in your ability to handle challenges.

Embark on this journey with dedication and patience. By incorporating these exercises and techniques into your life, you're actively cultivating unshakeable self-belief, paving the way for a more confident and empowered version of yourself post-breakup.

Challenging Limiting Beliefs After a Breakup: A Path to Healing

Understanding Limiting Beliefs
Limiting beliefs are the stories we tell ourselves, often ingrained in our minds, that hold us back from realizing our full potential. As explored in articles from hbr.org and thecouplescenter.org, these beliefs act as self-imposed barriers, shaping our perspectives and influencing our behavior.

Impact of Limiting Beliefs Post-Breakup
In the aftermath of a breakup, limiting beliefs can exacerbate the healing process. They cast shadows on your self-worth, hinder your ability to move forward and create barriers to building new, positive relationships. These beliefs often manifest as doubts about one's desirability, worthiness of love, or ability to trust again.

Steps to Overcoming Limiting Beliefs

Awareness is Key
The first step in challenging limiting beliefs is to become aware of them. Acknowledge the negative narratives playing in your mind. As Harvard Business Review suggests, mindfulness is crucial. Notice when these beliefs surface and their impact on your emotions and actions.

Think Critically About Your Values
Reflect on your values and beliefs. Are your current views aligned with who you are and aspire to be? The Couples Center encourages critical self-reflection to identify the origin and validity of these beliefs. Ensure your beliefs align with your core values and contribute positively to your growth.

Develop Your Senses
Engage your senses to challenge limiting beliefs. Harvard Business Review suggests tapping into sensory experiences to ground yourself in the present moment. This practice fosters a more objective perspective, allowing you to evaluate your beliefs from a balanced standpoint.

Think of Best-Case Scenarios
Challenge pessimistic beliefs by envisioning best-case scenarios. Consider the positive outcomes that can arise from embracing new possibilities. The Couples Center recommends visualizing a future where you've successfully moved past the limitations, allowing hope and optimism to replace self-imposed constraints.

Look for a Cue!
Identify cues that trigger limiting beliefs. According to Harvard Business Review, recognizing patterns in your thoughts and actions enables you to interrupt and redirect negative thinking. Establish cues that prompt you to challenge and reframe limiting beliefs, paving the way for a more positive mindset.

Optional Resource

If you find it beneficial, explore additional insights from goodmenproject.com. This resource may offer unique perspectives on overcoming breakup-inspired limiting beliefs, further enriching your journey toward healing and self-discovery.

Challenging limiting beliefs is a profound step in the process of post-breakup healing. By implementing these steps with dedication and self-compassion, you can dismantle the barriers that hold you back, fostering personal growth and resilience.

7
Reconnecting for New Beginnings

E mma's life had taken a devastating turn. At 28 years old, she had been on the brink of marrying the man she thought was the love of her life. They had plans for a beautiful wedding next year, but then she discovered the painful truth – her fiancé had been cheating on her. Heartbroken and betrayed, Emma had to call off the engagement and break up with him. The pain was unbearable, and it felt like her world was crumbling around her.

As if that wasn't enough to shatter her, Emma's life took another tragic turn when she lost her mother. The grief weighed heavy on her, and she felt like she was drowning in sorrow. She struggled to find a way to cope with the double loss, and her emotions were a turbulent storm of anger, sadness, and confusion.

During those dark days, Emma found herself unable to resist the temptation of digitally stalking her ex's social media. She tortured herself by watching him move on with his life, believing she had made a mistake by breaking up with him. She felt utterly alone and convinced no one would ever love her again. It was a painful cycle of self-doubt and despair.

Then, just when Emma thought things couldn't get any worse, a mutual friend dropped a bombshell – her ex had asked another woman to marry him only three months after their breakup. It was a gut-wrenching revelation that left her feeling utterly shattered. The pain was almost unbearable, but it also served as a wake-up call.

Emma knew she couldn't continue down this path of self-destruction. With immense determination, she sought help through self-help books and weekly therapy sessions. She dedicated time to her long-forgotten hobbies, like painting and hiking, rediscovering the joy they brought into her life. Slowly but steadily, she began to heal and rebuild.

Facing her challenges head-on, Emma emerged from the darkness a stronger and more resilient version of herself. She created new friendships, finding solace in the company of those who truly cared about her. Emma also managed to land her dream job, something she had always aspired to but never thought possible in the midst of her heartache. And, most importantly, she found a new love – someone who cherished and supported her in ways she had never imagined. Emma's journey through heartache and loss transformed her, proving that even in the depths of despair, there could be a path to recovery and a brighter future waiting ahead.

Self-Awareness in Relationships

A person can be required to take some steps backward after breaking up with someone to find another person again, but this isn't easy, as can be seen. Many of us have heard of taking our time before starting new relationships. But the question remains: So, what makes you sure that you are ready for it? However, this chapter should not fail to mention these symptoms, which should push you towards another relationship. Such self-exploration and self-realization are pathways towards developing new relationships.

What Is Self-Awareness?

Self-awareness encompasses knowing who one is, how one feels, what one wants, and what makes one move. Self-awareness refs to knowing yourself regarding the match between your expectations, feelings, and actions.

Types of Self-Awareness

- Public Self-awareness: The process entails consciousness about how we look before others. We follow social norms through it, but we tend to worry too much about what other people think about us.

- Private self-awareness: This is also referred to as the capacity for self-awareness and self-reflexivity. It puts it in our inner feelings and emotions.

Self-Awareness in New Relationships

- Healthy Relationship Patterns: Spotting your behavior and triggers of past relationships enables you to stop unhealthy behavioral patterns.

- Effective Communication: Self-awareness helps individuals express their limits and needs clearly, enabling them to build rapport and trust with their new partner.

- Compatibility Assessment: This includes understanding your values and goals and how they relate to potential partners for greater alignment.

- Personal Growth: Self-awareness motivates self-improvement, turning you into a perfect partner.

A Journey into Self-discovery

When it comes to relations, a world that nowadays starts and ends swipe, knowing the depth of your feelings and actions is mandatory. Chapter one is intended to be a roadmap that will prepare you for and guide you through a relationship that will survive beyond its "honeymoon" stage.

Picture You in a Perfect Relationship.

In a partnership, a picture is the ideal self. Consider what are the traits that you want to develop in yourself? and what kind of relationship you would like to establish with your partner. This is your north star, which will lead you through the kind of relationship you crave.

Ask the "What" Questions

Instead, change from saying, "Why am I like this?" to "What are the factors that cause my emotions or behaviors?" For instance, if you realize you are pulling away from relationships, query yourself, "What happened to me before from the past times?" The use of such an alternative way helps to recognize yourself.

Strengthen Your Emotional Intelligence

Train your brain to identify emotions and label them. For example, if an intense attack of anxiety hits you during a discussion on commitment, "I am anxious about commitment" will help you manage your emotions better.

Seek Feedback from Others

Find out what your close friends and past partners see you like in relationships. What have been their perceptions in terms of strengths and weaknesses? Your external viewpoint can pinpoint some of your qualities that you cannot notice.

Maintain a Relationship Journal

Record your daily sentiments and observations regarding your dating life. Ask yourself such questions as, "What triggered discomfort in me?" and "How did I feel after today's date?" These questions help to identify behavioral trends in dating.

Self-Awareness Gap in Relationships

Most of us think we know ourselves quite well, but accurate self-awareness is hardly always the case. In this context, it's easy to get trapped by patterns of denying or misunderstanding feelings. These gaps typically perpetuate cycles of unhealthy relations. These practices can close the gap and improve your ability to create genuine and satisfying relationships.

What is my sense of Self-Awareness?

Self-awareness is not an end but a progressive process. Taking periodic self-criticism and self-checks should help you determine how self-aware you are. Self-awareness should make you more aware of yourself and, thus, of other people. When you start applying these reflective practices, you give your emotions all the instruments necessary to sustain a positive and healthy relationship for the two of you. This chapter guides converting self-reflection into action that will lead you to more significant relationships.

The True Healing Symptoms after a Breakup

The First Step: Acceptance
At first, acceptance may appear as nothing more than just acting. Yet, it's a crucial step. It is possible to observe a case where you begin to put boundaries on things formerly blurred or set aside objects that link you with the past without grudges because they are useless for the current situation.

Clarity in Thought
Your mind does not always think about the breakup, as healing can also be seen in this regard. One experiences relief from mental fog that enables one to work, play, and talk with someone with clarity that had disappeared in the preceding period.

Blame Gives Way to Accountability

A typical defense mechanism involves blaming your ex or yourself, but as healing sets in, you start taking some responsibility for your happiness. Thus, it may imply quitting to retrace how people messed with you and reflect on what you learned from the experience.

Forgiveness as Freedom

Finally, forgiveness is a crucial step in the healing process. Forgetting does not mean you do not have to allow past hurts to dominate your chances of being happy in the future. That is when you think about your ex and don't get angry.

Flaws Become Features

You come to terms with yourself that even imperfections are not failures. They are unique aspects of you. You used to hide these things in yourself but will now find them as your own.

Embracing Change

Moreover, embracing Change is both a symbol and a fact of healing. The grace you acquire adapts you to new circumstances that were impossible before. You appreciate that change is not only imminent but mandatory for development.

The Confidence and Knowledge of Getting Back into the Dating Scene

However, in all healthy relationships, there must be a feeling of respect for each other, dialogue, and everyday pleasure from the company of the second person. Pillars of emotional connection, understanding, and personal growth and that of the couple nurture a good relationship. It is an association where they feel appreciated, listened to, and relate with each other.

Defining Relationship Compatibility

Essentially, compatibility seeks to create harmony whereby two unique individuals produce a more excellent song than what would be when apart. Despite every interest not matching, a couple flourishes on the grounds of mutual respect and equality, which fosters the same. Compatibility in a relationship, however, does not stop at similar interests on a surface level but goes down to the root level of sharing the same ideologies on life goals and the approach towards life and love.

Types of Compatibility

There are several facets to compatibility, each like a thread woven into the tapestry of a relationship:

- Emotional Compatibility: This forms the basis of any relationship. Simply put, it is the need to appreciate the emotional needs of our counterparts and reply compassionately.

- Intellectual Compatibility: Intellectual compatibility means having a shared level of curiosity towards the world, love for exchanging ideas, and respect for each other's opinions, even if they disagree.

- Sexual Compatibility: Not about mere sexual attractiveness but physical connection. This is about the urge to be intimate, the expression of the yearning, and the fulfillment of partners' desires to satisfy each other's sexual yearning.

- Lifestyle Compatibility: It is about how much two lives practically align, including everything from daily routines to life ambitions. Do you have a similar lifestyle? Do your career goals align? This is regarding the fitness of the lifestyle.

- Communication Compatibility: However, communication compatibility, which involves speaking and listening according to the understanding of both parties' feelings and opinions, is a critical element of any robust relationship.

The Importance of Compatibility
Why prioritize compatibility? Since it is the foundation of happiness in a relationship. If it is withheld from the couples, they will fight on different lines without wanting to be satisfied. Compatibility doesn't mean being identical but being together in ways that make a difference for mutual growth and satisfaction.

Finding Compatible Partners
Therefore, how do you find the right partner to get along with? Seek a person whom you really love their company and not because of titles or shallow things.

Astrology or even numerology could present exciting thoughts, but surely, your love quest should continue. However, the essential requirement is to believe in one's ability to change and develop despite the stars.

Compatibility in Every Aspect: Is it Necessary?

Seeking a perfect partner who ticks all boxes is unrealistic; however, some areas require more harmony than others. Compatibility regarding values, life goals, and conflict resolution strategies is essential. But always remember that some differences can strengthen a relationship as they may introduce every partner to a new look.

Signs of a Compatible Relationship

In recognizing a compatible relationship, you might notice:

Shared Values
Each of you will be speaking to the same fundamental beliefs and ethics.

Respectful Communication
Even in disagreement, you treat each other respectfully, talking and listening to one another.

Shared Interests
You have some shared interests and areas to relax and have fun together.

Trust
You both feel at ease as you are committed to one another.

Emotional Connection
In a nutshell, this means you understand each other's feelings and sympathize with each other.

10 Ways to Love Smart

1. **Evaluate Well-Being**
   Employ personal wellness as a point of reference. If you are feeling energized, have clear thoughts, and think that you can love better, then you are making good decisions with your choices.

2. **Express Emotions**
   Be honest about your feelings. You have to be authentic for one to understand and love you for what you are.

3. **Experience-Based Listening**
   Hear to understand and feel for your partner emotionally rather than merely with words.

4. **Provide Targeted Support**
   Know what your partner finds loving. Listen to their needs and don't make assumptions.

5. **Seek Clarity through Inquiry**
   Don't make assumptions; ask questions. Communication

must be direct for understanding to come.

6. **Commit to the Work**
Recognize that loving takes a lot of work. Attention makes relationships, and neglect kills them off.

7. **Learn Continuously**
Be open to learning from your partner. A relationship is a never-ending process of mutual growth.

8. **Be Mindful of Emotional Baggage**
Ensure that you are aware of how past injuries might affect your present impressions and responses.

9. **Own Your Mistakes**
Embrace errors as growth opportunities. The ability to admit one's mistakes is vital to a good relationship.

10. **Embrace Change Together**
Consider using the inevitably changing life as a chance for your relationship.

EQ, also known as emotional intelligence, is important because it forms the base of our ability to comprehend, interpret, and react to other people's emotions. EQ is more than academic or intellectual ability that helps us effectively cope with stress, enhance our relationships, and negotiate through the complexities of social intercourse.

Four Key Skills to Enhance Your EQ

1. Self-Management: Learn to regulate impulsive urges and emotions, initiate action and completion of tasks, and other skills necessary for effective functioning.

2. Self-awareness: Develop a keen sense of emotional

Intelligence to guide your decision-making and behavior.

3. Social Awareness: Increase your comprehension of body language and other people's emotions, developing empathy and social skills.

4. Relationship Management: Discover how to sustain healthy relations by communicating effectively and addressing issues of interpersonal dynamics.

Interactive Element: Create Your Healthy Relationship Framework

It is important to proceed carefully and to give yourself a minute's notice before starting a new romantic effort. Thus, use it as a chance to reflect on your previous relationships so that you can draw lessons from them and go into future ones with intention.

Remember that this method offers a framework for deliberate choice and change, not self-criticism.

Questions for Reflection

Responding to Stress and Conflict: How does your personality determine how to deal with disagreements or stressful moments in your relationship? What are some other approaches you can take towards healthy conflict resolution?

Acceptance vs Transformation: Are you ready to take someone the way s/he is without trying to make them what one idealizes as a perfect partner who fits one's idea of an ideal? How does the acceptance or non-acceptance of it determine your relationships?

Maintaining Individuality: Have you found yourself changing to suit their wants? What effect does this have on the genuineness of your encounters with people?

Emotional Mastery: Is it possible you are sometimes guided by the emotions rather than leading them yourself? If you work on improving your emotional regulation, how would this improve your future romantic life?

Communication Clarity: Your capacity to articulate your needs and wants. What has been the role of communication in building or destroying your previous relationships?

Self-Reflection on Contribution: Can you think of ways you could have made resolving any problems in your past or current relationship(s) more difficult? What lessons can you take away from these observations for future relationships?

In this essential chapter, we have handled the personal experiences of self-awareness and personal growth, crucial territories for those preparing to step back into the dating world. We've uncovered how to recognize the signs of readiness for a new romance and the profound role of understanding oneself in cultivating meaningful connections.

By reflecting on past relationships, you've learned to identify patterns in your romantic choices, respond positively to stress and conflict, and communicate your needs effectively. You've also considered the importance of maintaining authenticity and respecting your boundaries and your partner's.

8
A Final Reflection

"Time is the gentle hand that soothes the wounds of a broken heart, and grief is the storm that paves the way for a brighter tomorrow. In the embrace of time, we find healing, and in the depths of our grief, we discover our resilience to recover."

A s we end this journey together, I want you to take a moment to reflect on how far you've come. You've navigated the stormy seas of heartbreak and emerged stronger, wiser, and more resilient than ever before. This final chapter is not just an ending but a new beginning—a chance to embrace the incredible future that awaits you.

Throughout this book, we've delved into various aspects of healing a broken heart, from understanding the stages of relationship grief to the importance of communication, emotional responses, and seeking therapy when needed. You've gathered valuable insights and practical tools to help you on your healing journey. Now, it's time to put that knowledge into action and envision the beautiful life ahead.

Finding Your Inner Strength
Healing a broken heart is not a linear process; there may still be moments when the pain resurfaces. That's okay. Remember, healing is not about erasing the past but finding the strength to

move forward despite it. You are stronger than you think, and your capacity for resilience is boundless. Draw upon your inner strength, and let it guide you through the most challenging times.

The Power of Self-Compassion

One of the most profound ways to heal is through self-compassion. Be gentle with yourself, as you would with a dear friend going through a difficult time. Acknowledge your feelings, and don't judge yourself for them. It's natural to experience a wide range of emotions during the healing process, and every emotion is valid.

Practice self-care regularly. Engage in activities that nourish your soul, whether yoga, meditation, journaling, or simply taking long walks in nature. Treating yourself with kindness and prioritizing your well-being creates a strong foundation for moving forward.

Cultivating a Positive Mindset

Your thoughts have a tremendous impact on your emotional well-being. Challenge negative thought patterns and replace them with positive affirmations. Remind yourself of your worth, strengths, and potential for happiness. Surround yourself with positivity and people who uplift you.

Visualize the life you want to create. What does it look like? What are your goals and dreams? By focusing on a bright and hopeful future, you'll naturally gravitate toward opportunities that align with your vision.

Embracing Change and Growth

Heartbreak often catalyzes personal growth and transformation. Use this time to rediscover yourself. What were your passions and interests before the relationship? Reconnect with hobbies and activities that bring you joy. Explore new experiences and challenge yourself to step out of your comfort zone.

Remember that life is a journey filled with ups and downs, and change is inevitable. Embrace transformation as an opportunity for growth and evolution. Each day is a chance to learn, to become stronger, and to move closer to the person you aspire to be.

Building Healthy Relationships

As you heal and move forward, you may find yourself open to new relationships. When the time is right, approach them with self-awareness and healthy boundaries. You deserve a partner who respects and values you, just as you should respect and love yourself.

Effective communication, as we discussed earlier, is crucial in any relationship. Share your feelings and expectations openly, and encourage your partner to do the same. Healthy relationships are built on trust, respect, and mutual support.

The Role of Therapy and Support

If you haven't already, consider seeking therapy or counseling to aid your healing process further. A trained professional can provide guidance, tools, and a safe space to explore your emotions and experiences. Remember that seeking help is a sign of strength, not weakness.

Additionally, lean on the support of friends and loved ones who have been there for you throughout this journey. Share your progress with them, and let their love and encouragement lift you.

Gratitude and Forgiveness

One of the most potent acts of healing is forgiveness—not only of your ex-partner but also of yourself. Holding onto resentment and anger only prolongs the pain. Instead, focus on the lessons you've learned and the growth you've experienced. Find gratitude in the small moments and the people who have supported you.

Forgiveness is a gift you give yourself. It frees you from the chains of the past and allows you to embrace the present and future fully.

Your Bright Future Awaits

As we conclude this chapter and this book, I want you to know that your future is filled with infinite possibilities. You are a resilient, courageous, and beautiful soul with much to offer. You have the strength to heal, grow, and create a life that brings you joy and fulfillment.

The pain of a broken heart may linger, but it will no longer define you. You are not broken but a mosaic of experiences, emotions, and strengths. With time, patience, and self-love, you will heal and thrive.

Your heart may have been wounded, but it has also been opened to the beauty of life's journey. Embrace this journey with open arms, for it is through healing that we discover our most authentic selves and the extraordinary possibilities that lie ahead.

Show Your Support By Sharing

I hope you've been enjoying your journey through the pages of this book so far. As an author, my primary goal is to provide you with valuable insights, knowledge, or entertainment. Your feedback is incredibly important to me, as it helps me understand whether I've achieved that goal. Are you finding the content useful, thought-provoking, or simply enjoyable? Your opinions matter!

If you've been finding value in this book, I kindly request that you consider leaving a review. Your review can make a world of difference for other potential readers who are trying to decide if this book is the right fit for them. Your honest thoughts and opinions can guide them in making an informed choice. It's a small gesture that can have a big impact, and I genuinely appreciate your support. Thank you for being a part of this literary journey, and I look forward to hearing your thoughts.

Thank you for embarking on this healing journey with me. I believe in you and am excited to see your fantastic future.

With love and hope,

Krista Cantell

Made in the USA
Las Vegas, NV
20 April 2024

88957934R00075